MANAGED CARE
MADE EASY

Other Books From the People's Medical Society

Getting the Most for Your Medical Dollar

Long-Term Care and Its Alternatives

Massage Made Easy

Medicare Made Easy

Medicine on Trial

So You're Going to Be a Mother

Take This Book to the Gynecologist With You

Take This Book to the Hospital With You

Take This Book to the Pediatrician With You

The Complete Book of Relaxation Techniques

The Hormone Replacement Handbook

The Savvy Medical Consumer

Yoga Made Easy

Your Medical Rights

MANAGED CARE MADE EASY

by Vikram Khanna

≡People's Medical Society®

Allentown, Pennsylvania

The People's Medical Society is a nonprofit consumer health organization dedicated to the principles of better, more responsive and less expensive medical care. Organized in 1983, the People's Medical Society puts previously unavailable medical information into the hands of consumers so that they can make informed decisions about their own health care.

Membership in the People's Medical Society is $20 a year and includes a subscription to the *People's Medical Society Newsletter.* For information, write to the People's Medical Society, 462 Walnut Street, Allentown, PA 18102, or call 610-770-1670.

This and other People's Medical Society publications are available for quantity purchase at discount. Contact the People's Medical Society for details.

© 1997 by Vikram Khanna
Printed in the United States of America

Library of Congress Cataloging-in-Publication Data
Khanna, Vikram.
    Managed care made easy / by Vikram Khanna.
       p.   cm.
    Includes index.
    ISBN 1-882606-26-4
    1. Managed care plans (Medical care)—United States.
2. Consumer education. I. Title.
RA413.5.U5K49   1997
362.1'04258'0973—dc21   97-28567
                                     CIP

1 2 3 4 5 6 7 8 9 0
First printing, September 1997

For my mother, Gyan,
and my late father, Prem

CONTENTS

FOREWORD 13

ACKNOWLEDGMENTS 17

1 What Is Managed Care and Why Should You Care? 21

Managed Care: What It Is and How It Differs
From Fee-For-Service Health Care 22

Why You Should Care About Managed Care 25

Understanding the Various Types of
Managed Care 30

Features Common to All Managed
Care Programs 32

Different Kinds of HMOs 34

Other Aspects of Managed Care 39

2 Understanding the Advantages and Disadvantages of Managed Care 41

How Managed Care Can Improve
All Health-Care Delivery 41

Advantages and Disadvantages of Managed Care 44

Advantages of HMOs 45

Controversies Surrounding Managed Care 52

For-Profit Versus Not-For-Profit
Managed Care Plans 57

How Managed Care Affects the Way
Health-Care Providers Work 60

3 Selecting Your Managed Care Plan 65

Defining Your Goals 67

Getting Information on Your
Managed Care Options 68

Managed Care Plan Accreditation 70

National Committee for
Quality Assurance (NCQA) 72

Joint Commission on Accreditation of
Healthcare Organizations (JCAHO) 74

American Accreditation Healthcare
Commission (AAHC) 76

Choosing a Managed Care Plan 77

4 Picking Your Doctor in Managed Care 95

Understanding the Relationship Between
Doctors and Managed Care Plans 98

Getting Started 102

Choosing a Primary Care Doctor 104

Choosing a Specialist 114

Making the Transition to a New Doctor 120

5 Getting the Most From Managed Care 125

The Basics 125

Managed Care and Preventive Health Care 128

Managed Care and Acute Illness 134

Managed Care and Chronic Illness 136

Managed Care and Emergencies 140

Managed Care and Hospital Services 142

Managed Care and Pregnancy 147

Managed Care and Children 148

6 Using Managed Care to Meet Special Needs 151

Managed Care and Mental Health Care 151

Managed Care and Vision and Dental Care 153

Vision Care 153

Dental Care 154

Managed Care and Prescription Drugs 155

Managed Care and Illnesses Away From Home 157

Managed Care and Ancillary Services 160

Managed Care and the End of Life 160

Managed Care and Alternative Medicine 161

7 Fixing Problems in Managed Care 163

Using the Plan's Customer Service Department 164

When and How to File a Written Complaint
With Your Managed Care Plan 166

Preparing Your Grievance or Appeal 167

*Complaint-Resolution Tips for
Medicare HMO Enrollees* 173

*Complaint-Resolution Tips for
Medicaid HMO Enrollees* 175

Getting Help From State Government Agencies 176

Getting Help for Complaints Against
Self-Insured Managed Care Plans 178

EPILOGUE
Using Managed Care Wisely and
Making the System Work 181

APPENDIX A
State Attorney Generals' Offices 185

APPENDIX B
State Health Departments 191

APPENDIX C
State Insurance Departments 197

APPENDIX D
Health Insurance Information
and Counseling 203

GLOSSARY 207

INDEX 225

FOREWORD

Not long ago, I gave a speech to a hall full of union members. I talked about managed care—you know, health maintenance organizations (HMOs) and the like. A man in the audience stood up and said he would have nothing to do with managed care— ever. But when I asked him about his current insurance, I discovered that he was enrolled in managed care without even knowing it. And the fact is, so are millions of other Americans.

If your health insurance policy requires that you get prior approval for a test, treatment or operation, that's managed care. If your employer provides coverage for medications but specifies certain pharmacies where the prescriptions must be filled, that's managed care. If your insurance covers hospitalization for mental illness but limits it to a certain number of days, that, too, is managed care.

In other words, any time your health insurance limits your choices, provides incentives such as no out-of-pocket payments to use certain providers or dictates where you can go for care, you are a part of managed care.

Managed care is growing rapidly. And clearly, it is here to stay. Yet for most consumers, it is a hodgepodge of complicated terms, confusing rules and difficult choices. While *managed care* is nothing more than a general term applied to a variety of health insurance models, those models are new and unlike any form of insurance most of us have ever owned. No wonder, then, that my union friend was confused. And from my experience, he's not the only person who is having a hard time figuring out managed care.

Consumer reviews on managed care are mixed. Polls show that people in managed care programs generally like them. However, the more restrictive a plan is, the higher the level of dissatisfaction. In surveys of people who have quit managed care plans, the number one reason cited is the plan's failure to live up to its promises. Another major complaint is poor customer service.

Yet managed care can be a blessing for many people. For a senior citizen on Medicare who cannot afford supplemental insurance and does not want to deal with any paperwork, a Medicare HMO may be just the thing. For a young family with a child who suffers from asthma, the asthma management program in a particular managed care plan may keep the condition under control with few hassles and bring peace of mind to worried parents. And since managed care comes in many forms, from very restrictive HMOs to point-of-service plans that allow a person to use any doctor (whether under contract to the plan or not), there is probably an option for everyone.

Here at the People's Medical Society, we have been fielding consumer's questions about managed care for many years. As far back as 1985, we published a small publication titled *The ABCs of HMOs*. It was one of our most popular publications. But in recent years, the number of inquiries has increased dramatically. And so have the number and types of managed care plans. Therefore, we feel it is important that consumers have a book that gives them all the information they need to understand and use managed care. And this is that book.

Managed Care Made Easy is your one-stop guide to managed care. Its goal is to make managed care understandable and to empower the consumer to get the most out of any managed care program. I think that goal has been accomplished. From describing the various managed care models to helping you select a plan, choose doctors within the plan and know how to avoid managed care pitfalls, *Managed Care Made Easy* takes the guesswork out of making important health-care decisions. It serves as your handbook as you ponder your health insurance options.

Like all People's Medical Society books, *Managed Care Made Easy* is written for you, the consumer. We are not promoting managed care or putting it down. We talk about what makes managed care good and what can go wrong. We warn you of the common problems you might encounter and how to avoid them. And most important, we provide you with the information you'll need to make the right managed care decisions.

Managed care can work for you, but you're going to have to do a little work to make that happen. And frankly, that little bit of work will ensure that you are getting the best health and medical treatment available, when you need it, from the most qualified providers of care, at a price you can afford.

So don't let managed care overwhelm you. If you use *Managed Care Made Easy* as your guide, you'll be in control of your own health care. And that's a goal we should all strive to reach.

CHARLES B. INLANDER
President
People's Medical Society
Allentown, Pennsylvania

ACKNOWLEDGMENTS

This book would not be complete if I did not express my deep gratitude to mentors, friends and colleagues.

To the finest public servants I know, whose leadership makes a difference in the lives of health-care consumers every day: Maryland Attorney General Joe Curran, Maryland State Senator Tom Bromwell, and Assistant Attorney Generals Hank Greenberg, Bill Leibovici and Jack Schwartz.

To the friends of a lifetime, whose support for me and my various escapades never falters: Bob Bollinger, Ralph Boyd, Paul H. Daby, Laura and Rich Gurdak, Ilene Heaney, Karla and Jim Leap, Rich Pfau, Elisa and Paul Rusonis and Steve Teret. And a special note of thanks to Bob Westerfield and Nicole McGehee, the first two people to read the outline for this book. Their infectious enthusiasm and savvy about health care and publishing helped convince me to write it. I also owe a debt of gratitude, which I can never fully repay, to the late J. Michael McGehee, a trusted friend and colleague who died far too soon.

And last but not least, to Karla Morales and Charles Inlander of the People's Medical Society, for their patience, guidance, friendship and wisdom. You are the best.

MANAGED CARE MADE EASY

Terms printed in boldface can be found in the glossary,
beginning on page 207. Only the first mention of the word
in the text will be boldfaced.

We have tried to use male and female pronouns in an
egalitarian manner throughout the book. Any imbalance
in usage has been in the interest of readability.

1 What Is Managed Care and Why Should You Care?

Our health-care system has undergone many dramatic changes in the past 50 to 60 years. We have seen the development of lifesaving drugs and technologies, as well as rapid growth in the number and kinds of health-care professionals who diagnose and treat disease. The way health care is delivered and paid for has also changed. The most important change in health-care financing and delivery is the growth of **managed care** as a form of health insurance for consumers.

For many consumers, managed care is a relatively new concept. Nonetheless, it is something that you will probably face at some time. It is important for you to understand what it is and how it works. Most consumers will come into contact with managed care at their jobs because most of us get our health insurance through our employers. Consumers who buy their health insurance as individuals also have the option to choose managed care instead of **traditional indemnity** (or **fee-for-service**) **insurance** plans. Indemnity insurance is a pay-as-you-go process that many consumers are accustomed to, where they receive doctor or hospital care, and their insurers pay the bills.

Fewer and fewer Americans are enrolled in traditional

indemnity insurance plans. Rather, if you are shopping for health insurance today, you will likely choose from some form of managed care as your way of getting health insurance.

Increasing numbers of consumers who receive their health-care benefits through **Medicare** or **Medicaid**, the two major government-sponsored health insurance programs, are also enrolling in managed care to get their health-care services. State governments are placing Medicaid recipients in a form of managed care called **health maintenance organizations (HMOs)**. And the federal government is both offering and encouraging Medicare beneficiaries to join HMOs rather than stay in traditional Medicare. The federal government believes that by enrolling senior citizens in managed care, it can help slow the rate of growth in Medicare spending.

Because it is now so widespread in our health-care system, you need to know about managed care and how it works to make it work for you. The more informed you are, the more likely it is that managed care will meet your whole family's needs. So let's start with the basics.

MANAGED CARE: WHAT IT IS AND HOW IT DIFFERS FROM FEE-FOR-SERVICE HEALTH CARE

Managed care is a philosophy about how to deliver and pay for health care. It's a broad term that describes several ways to deliver and pay for health care using many different kinds of companies, organizations and plans. Managed care's most important feature is that it combines paying for and providing health-care services into one more tightly controlled system than most health-care consumers are accustomed to.

The goal of managed care is to make sure that consumers have access to appropriate, high-quality health care at a reasonable cost. Managed care also tries to control health-care spending by consumers, employers and government. It does this by studying and eliminating health-care services (tests and surgical procedures, for example) that are unnecessary, unproven or not cost-effective and by increasing the role of **preventive health-care** services that help keep people from getting sick or delay the onset of illness. This is what makes managed care very different from the traditional indemnity insurance you have now or have had in the past (see page 24).

There are important distinctions between traditional indemnity insurance and managed care. The word *indemnity* literally means compensation or payment for something. Traditional indemnity insurance typically pays for a consumer's health care on a service-by-service basis, after the consumer receives the care.

In most cases, traditional indemnity insurance companies do not take the time to question whether the bills are too high (since the company pays a provider a discounted amount other than the total shown on the bill) or whether the services you received were appropriate for your diagnosis. All they do is make sure the services you received are covered under the plan and pay the provider an agreed-upon fee. Also, if traditional indemnity insurance plans experience higher costs for services, they simply pass along those costs to their customers—the consumers and employers who purchased their insurance—in the form of higher **premiums** in subsequent years.

In the pay-as-you-go scheme of traditional indemnity insurance plans, it is easy, and lucrative, for doctors to order more tests and perform more services because they know they will get paid with few questions asked. Doctors can easily refer their patients to specialists because there are few—if any—rules governing **referrals**. It is also easy for a consumer to go to a specialist without first seeing his family doctor for a recommendation and with little concern for the cost of the visit to the higher-priced specialist. With traditional indemnity insurance, the consumer knows that the insurance company will pay the bulk, if not all, of a

TRADITIONAL INDEMNITY INSURANCE

Here is how traditional indemnity insurance works.

• You see your doctor for an office visit. In a traditional indemnity insurance plan, you can go to the doctor of your choice at any time. It does not matter whether the doctor you see has a contract with your indemnity insurance plan. (Using a doctor who has a contract with the plan may, however, have some advantages for you, such as a lower **copayment**.)

• The doctor provides services, tests and procedures that he thinks are appropriate. He may also recommend that you see a **specialist** for an additional evaluation. A specialist is a physician who has training and expertise in a specific field of medicine that goes beyond the training and expertise of a **primary care physician**.

• Your doctor, the lab that does the testing and the specialist you see all prepare bills, which either are paid by you or go from the **providers** to your insurance company for payment.

• Your insurance company reviews the bills and, in most cases, pays them with little question. The insurance company sends its payments to you, the lab or your doctors. Where the payment goes depends on the precise nature of the contract you and the health-care providers have with the insurance company.

• Usually, you pay a copayment or have to spend a certain amount of money each year (a **deductible**) before your indemnity insurance makes any payments.

specialist's bills, generally with little hassle or question about whether a specialist was needed.

Historically, traditional indemnity insurance contributed to high health-care costs because it rewarded doctors for doing more, even if additional services were unnecessary. It also encouraged the use of specialists, who were more likely to perform expensive procedures such as a test or a surgical procedure than were **family physicians** and other general physicians. Specialists nearly always charge more money for their services than do family physicians or other primary care physicians. In fact, specialists typically charge more than primary care physicians for the same procedure (for example, performing a minor in-office surgical procedure).

Specialty physicians have not demonstrated through scientific studies that consumers benefit from having them perform simple diagnostic or treatment procedures that less expensive physicians could do as well. Conversely, however, specialists should always perform certain tests and procedures because their advanced training leads to fewer complications and better outcomes for consumers.

The challenge for managed care plans is not only to ensure that consumers have appropriate access to specialists when necessary but also to manage the costs and utilization of high-tech specialty services to reduce the performance of procedures without clear benefit.

WHY YOU SHOULD CARE ABOUT MANAGED CARE

Managed care is not a new concept. Its roots go back more than 50 years, when some large employers wanted to provide their employees with medical care and simultaneously control the cost and quality of the services. Managed care did not take off in a big way until medical inflation soared in the 1980s. By then, both employers and the federal government faced staggering annual increases in their medical costs.

All managed care is not the same. Quality varies from plan to plan and across providers within some plans. The savvy medical consumer is a person who knows what to look for when choosing a managed care plan and how to make the plan work for him once enrolled. Polls show that most consumers do not know very much about managed care. Polls also indicate that consumers in managed care plans are generally as satisfied with their care as consumers who are not in managed care. This changes, however, when consumers are confronted with serious illness. Then consumer satisfaction with managed care drops. Recent studies also raise questions about how well consumers with serious illnesses fare in managed care. These are the real tests of a managed care plan's quality and commitment to its consumers. But if you do your homework in advance and play an active role in your health care, chances are that you will do well in managed care. In essence, it is up to you to manage managed care.

Managed care emphasizes careful planning of health-care services to better coordinate how and where consumers get their care. Planning and coordination help control health-care spending by ensuring that care is delivered by the most appropriate health-care professionals, using the most appropriate tests and treatments, in the settings that are best for the consumers.

For example, a consumer with mild hypertension (high blood pressure) that is successfully managed with either drugs or diet and exercise does not usually need to see a cardiologist for regular checkups. In a managed care plan, this consumer would see a primary care provider (a physician, **physician assistant** or **nurse practitioner**) for routine checkups. The consumer would see a cardiologist only if there were complications, new **symptoms** or other problems related to the high blood pressure that required the expertise and training of a cardiologist. And the primary care provider is less expensive and is well prepared to take care of this consumer.

On the other hand, in the traditional indemnity insurance system, the consumer could see a cardiologist for management of his stable high blood pressure—likely without any measurable benefit—and the insurer would probably pay for the additional expense and not raise a question about the need for such high-level or expensive care.

In managed care, consumers are directed to use some services (such as one particular laboratory for blood tests) and not use others (such as pharmacies that do not agree to dispense prescription drugs at the managed care plan's rates). By taking these steps and others that we will discuss later, managed care changes how you interact with and think about health-care providers, including doctors, hospitals, labs and others.

Just like traditional indemnity insurance plans, managed care plans have rules. But there tend to be more rules in a managed care plan, and the consequences of not following them are usually more severe. Managed care's rules cover a wide range of issues—from limiting whom you can select and use as your doctor to who decides how long you stay in the hospital after surgery and what kinds of prescription drugs you can use. There are financial penalties if you break managed care rules. In other words, if you do not abide by the managed care plan's rules and use the services it provides, you will have to pay for your care **out-of-pocket**.

Some managed care plans also want to limit what you learn about your health-care options. There are some things that most managed care plans and managed care companies don't want you to know about, such as rules in the companies' contracts with physicians that can keep your doctor from telling you some of the options available for diagnosing and treating an illness. These are called **gag rules**. Gag rules are intended to keep the terms and provisions of the contract between the managed care plan and a doctor completely private.

For example, the managed care plan may not want you to know that physicians can get bonuses for making fewer referrals to specialists. Or it may not want you to know that it does not want to encourage certain operations on people over a certain age.

By having gag rules, a managed care plan keeps you from learning how it has decided what care it may allow or not allow in your situation. Plans can decide not to cover or pay for a test or treatment for many reasons: It is too expensive, its medical value is unproven, or the plan believes that the new test or therapy is not significantly better than another approach—or a combination of all these reasons. Gag rules tend to keep consumers from making informed choices about treatment and testing decisions because they do not get all the information they need. They also put doctors in a very awkward position. While your doctor has a legal and ethical obligation to inform you about all the options that are available for your care, he is also working under a contract with a managed care company that pays his bills and sets the rules. Obviously, there is a potential conflict of interest.

Managed care is a form of health insurance. No matter what the exact model of managed care, the goals are the same. Managed care is designed to provide your health care at a lower cost than traditional indemnity insurance. Physicians in managed care are paid salaries, reduced fees for each service they provide (compared with the fees paid by traditional indemnity insurance plans) or fixed monthly fees no matter how many visits you make. Therefore, in managed care there is less incentive to provide unnecessary services. On the other hand, both the doctors and the managed care plans make more money when consumers use fewer services. Ideally, consumers in managed care plans use fewer services because managed care plans help them stay healthy through services that help prevent illness, delay its onset or catch it early when it is easier to treat. There are concerns about whether managed care plans and the doctors in them achieve these goals or whether they deny needed services to some consumers simply to save money.

GAG RULES

Many state legislatures have passed laws that make it illegal for managed care plans to put gag rules in their contracts with doctors. Managed care plans say that their contracts never contained gag rules and that the debate over gag rules was just something doctors and consumers made up to attack managed care plans. This is not true. In October 1996, Humana, which operates managed care plans around the country, announced that it was removing gag rules from all the contracts it signs with doctors. And in December 1996, Medicare sent a letter to all 300 managed care plans that serve Medicare enrollees and said it would not tolerate any kind of gag rules.

To make sure that you get all the information you need, ask these questions when you discuss treatment or testing options with your doctor.

• "Have you told me everything that in your professional judgment I need to know to make an informed choice about what tests or treatments to have?"

• "Does my managed care plan limit what you can tell me about my options?"

• "Are there any other options that I should know about, regardless of whether my managed care plan will pay for them or not?"

Overall, however, there are reasons for consumers to like managed care. Consumers in managed care benefit from high levels of coverage, the security of knowing what their medical costs will be for a full year and the plan's emphasis on prevention. Things they dislike include limited choices of health care providers and difficulty getting access to specialists.

UNDERSTANDING THE VARIOUS TYPES OF MANAGED CARE

There are several types of managed care programs. HMOs— which we've already mentioned briefly—**preferred provider organizations (PPOs)** and **point-of-service (POS)** plans are the most popular forms of managed care. There are also **physician hospital organizations (PHOs), Medicare HMOS** and **Medicaid HMOs**.

• HMOs are the oldest and easiest type of managed care to understand. There are now nearly 600 HMOs across the United States. Some are for-profit corporations, while others are not-for-profit entities. As an HMO member, you or your employer pays the HMO a monthly premium. For that premium, you receive all the medical care you need as covered by the plan. That includes both physician and hospital services. HMOs typically cover and pay for some services that traditional indemnity insurance plans often do not cover and pay for, such as immunizations, mammograms and **well-baby care**. In exchange for getting this wide range of services, HMO members agree to use physicians and hospitals affiliated with or employed by the HMO. If at any time you use a doctor or hospital not affiliated with the HMO, you will likely pay for all or part of the cost of that service yourself. The only exceptions are in certain emergency situations.

• PPOs are very similar to HMOs. Typically, they are large networks of doctors and hospitals that are organized and owned by insurance companies or the doctors and hospitals in the PPO.

PPOs usually offer consumers more choices of doctors and hospitals than are available in HMOs, and consumers in PPOs generally have more freedom to see the doctors of their choice whenever they wish. Nearly 90 million American belong to PPOs.

• A POS plan is a cross between an HMO and a traditional indemnity insurance plan. In fact, POS is the best of both worlds and one of the most rapidly growing aspects of managed care. If a consumer in a POS plan uses the doctors or hospitals in the plan's network (the HMO "side" of a POS plan), he pays nothing or a small copayment for each visit. If he uses a doctor or hospital not in the plan's network (the traditional indemnity "side" of the POS plan), he pays a greater share of the cost of the service. However, the POS plan pays a significant portion of a consumer's bill, typically 60 to 70 percent, if nonplan providers are used. And while the consumer pays the other 30 to 40 percent, the total outlay a person pays in a year is generally capped at anywhere from $1,000 to $2,500. Once a consumer reaches the annual cap, the POS plan pays all the bills for covered services.

• PHOs are a recent addition to managed care. Typically, they are owned by their member doctors and hospitals. PHOs are relatively few in number, and they vary in how many providers are affiliated with them. The doctors and hospitals in PHOs share resources such as administrative functions (**claims** processing, for example). PHOs can contract with HMOs to treat its members. Or PHOs can, depending on state laws, compete directly with HMOs and sign up consumers directly without having to first work with HMOs.

• Medicare and Medicaid HMOs are exactly what their names imply: HMOs that are approved by federal and state governments for Medicare and Medicaid beneficiaries.

We will look more closely at the various kinds of managed care models soon. But first, let's examine the major features common in all managed care programs.

FEATURES COMMON TO ALL
MANAGED CARE PROGRAMS

HMOs and PPOs provide services to their enrollees (known as members) through **networks of health-care providers**— hospitals and doctors who are selected and contracted by an HMO or PPO to treat members. When you enroll in an HMO or PPO, you generally get all your services through the network of providers who work with the plan you've chosen.

Another common element of managed care is its emphasis on primary care physicians. The primary care provider is usually a family physician, an **internist**, a **pediatrician** or an **obstetrician/gynecologist**. The primary care provider is responsible for giving you most of your basic health-care services, such as preventive health care and routine checkups, and for treating a wide range of illnesses and injuries. The primary care provider also controls your access to other health-care providers who work with the plan. In this capacity, the primary care provider is a **gatekeeper**. That is, he controls the access—or the gate—through which you are referred to see specialists in the plan, undergo tests and other diagnostic services or get admitted to the hospital.

The primary care provider is the doctor you go to for referral to a specialist in the plan. In some managed care plans, you even need a referral for some routine care, such as an eye exam. In most plans, you or your primary care provider can choose a specialist from a list of doctors who work with the plan. Managed care plans generally sign contracts with only a few specialists in a medical field (such as cardiology or ophthalmology) in each locality. If you go to a specialist without a referral from your primary care provider, your plan will probably not cover or pay for that service. This will also happen if you see a specialist who is not under contract with the plan you belong to. So going to a specialist without a referral is potentially a very expensive matter. Some managed care plans are changing their rules on seeing specialists, however. They allow a consumer to see any specialist in the plan's network at any time for a slightly higher copayment than if he got a referral from the primary care provider.

A POS plan gives consumers additional flexibility to see the health-care providers of their choice. In some states, managed care plans must, by law, offer their members a POS option. A POS plan works like this.

• You need or want to see a specialist for blurry vision.

• In a managed care plan with a POS option, you have two choices. First, you can go to your primary care provider and get a referral to an eye specialist (**ophthalmologist**) who is in the plan's network (the HMO or PPO "side" of the POS option). Or second, you can go to the ophthalmologist of your choice, whether or not he is a member of the HMO network (the traditional indemnity "side" of the POS option).

• By going through your primary care provider to an eye doctor who has a contract with the plan, you usually pay no or little money out of your pocket for the visit.

• If you go to another eye doctor without a referral from your primary care physician, you pay a significant percentage of the charges out of your own pocket. Your plan, however, still pays for part of the visit. How much the plan pays depends on the specific details in your contract and may also vary by the laws of your state.

If your managed care plan does not have a POS option, you will not get any money from the plan for your visit to the out-of-network eye doctor. So while a POS option forces consumers to pay higher out-of-pocket costs than if they stayed in the network for their care, it saves money for consumers who go out of the network. And a POS plan allows the consumer full freedom of choice in providers.

One potential disadvantage of a POS plan is that if you go out of the plan's network for your visit to the eye doctor, you may need to file a claim to get reimbursed for the cost of the visit. So there is paperwork that you would not have to complete if you went to an eye doctor in the plan's network.

Unlike HMOs, most PPOs allow consumers to go to a specialist without a referral from another physician, as long as the specialist is in the PPO's network. If the specialist is not in the PPO's network, then you will likely pay more for the visit.

DIFFERENT KINDS OF HMOs

The 600 HMOs around the United States have about 60 million members. There are six basic HMO models, which differ mostly in how they set up their health-care networks and how they pay their hospitals and doctors.

• **Staff model HMO.** In this model, the HMO employs physicians and pays them salaries. The physicians may also receive bonuses if the HMO does well financially. The HMO generally owns the clinics and offices where consumers receive services. Doctors in a staff model HMO usually do not see patients who are not members of the HMO. Because of this, the HMO is said to have a **closed panel** of physicians who treat only HMO consumers. Some staff model HMOs own their own hospitals as well, but in most cases, they sign contracts with local hospitals to which they admit plan members. According to the American Association of Health Plans (AAHP), a Washington trade group that represents the interests of managed care plans, there are 54 staff model HMOs in the United States.

• **Group model HMO.** This model usually signs a contract with one or more large, independently owned groups of physicians to provide care to HMO members. These doctors are not salaried employees of the HMO but are employed by their group.

The group owns its offices and may have several locations in an area. The doctors' group may receive a fee from the HMO for each service it provides. Or the HMO may pay the group a set amount each month for each HMO enrollee that selects a doctor in the group as his primary care physician. This latter financial arrangement is called **capitation**. Under capitation, the doctors' group receives a fixed fee each month to provide care for the consumers in the HMO who use the group's doctors. We will discuss capitation in detail later in the book. Doctors in a group model HMO may contract with any number of HMOs and, therefore, see consumers who belong to many different plans. They may also see consumers who use traditional indemnity health insurance or pay for their care out-of-pocket. When doctors see consumers from a variety of health insurance plans and options, it is called an **open panel**. According to the AAHP, there are 57 group model HMOs in the United States.

• **Independent practice association (IPA).** In this HMO model, the plan's administrators sign contracts with large numbers of physicians—both solo practice doctors and doctors in group practices—to provide care to the HMO's members. Like the group model HMO, the doctors in an IPA are frequently paid through capitation, often with incentive bonuses. For example, physicians who meet the plan's target for the maximum number of **inpatient** hospital admissions would get bonuses, and those who exceed the target would not.

IPAs are usually open panel because the doctors who work in IPAs have contracts with other HMOs, PPOs and traditional indemnity insurance plans. IPAs are the most common kind of HMO in the United States, with 369 plans.

• **Mixed model** (or **network**) **HMO.** This model has a mix of all the different models incorporated into one plan. The managed care plan's administrators sign contracts with solo physicians and groups of doctors and may also employ some doctors.

Mixed model HMOs are typically open panel. There are about 94 network or mixed model HMOs in the United States.

• **Medicaid HMOs.** These HMOs serve persons with low incomes who are in state-run Medicaid programs. Medicaid programs around the country are moving large numbers of their enrollees into HMOs in an effort to provide more comprehensive services and save money. Some HMOs that enroll Medicaid recipients serve only Medicaid recipients. Others serve Medicaid and non-Medicaid consumers. Thus, a Medicaid HMO can be either open panel or closed panel. Each state implements its own program of Medicaid HMOs (see page 38).

• **Medicare HMOs.** This HMO model works with the federal Medicare program, which provides health insurance for nearly all persons in the United States age 65 or older and many disabled persons. Medicare HMOs also can be either open panel or closed panel.

MEDICARE HMOs

If you are enrolled in the federal Medicare program, you will face many of the same issues as other consumers joining managed care plans. The guidelines in this book will help you select the best program.

Medicare enrollees have some special issues to consider and be aware of before joining a Medicare health maintenance organization (HMO). Managed care plans that serve Medicare enrollees must sign a contract with the federal Medicare program and meet certain standards. You can join a Medicare HMO if you live in an area where at least one plan has a contract with Medicare.

continued

- Medicare enrollees who are receiving **hospice care** or treatment for end-stage renal disease *cannot* join a Medicare HMO.
- You must be enrolled in Medicare Part B to join a Medicare HMO. You will continue to pay the monthly premium for Part B—$43.80 in 1997—while you are in the Medicare HMO.
- You may have other costs in a Medicare HMO. For example, Medicare HMOs can charge enrollees a monthly premium (usually $50 to $75 per month) if they provide services beyond what Medicare normally covers. They may also charge a copayment (usually $5 to $15) for doctor visits.
- Medicare HMOs must provide at least the same services to enrollees that are provided in the traditional Medicare program. Some Medicare HMOs offer extra services, too. These often include limited coverage for prescription drugs or eyeglasses, which the Medicare program does not cover.
- You can join or leave a Medicare HMO at any time. You must, however, do this in writing (using a form provided by the HMO) and give the form to the HMO.
- If your Medicare HMO ever denies you services that you believe it should cover, you can **appeal** the decision.
- Every state has a hotline number that Medicare enrollees can call to get more information about what managed care plans are in their areas. You can also call this number to get help if you have a problem with a Medicare HMO, to report wrongdoing or to get help understanding the differences between plans. (See Appendix D for a list of phone numbers.)

MEDICAID HMOs

In many states, managed care plans such as health maintenance organizations (HMOs) approach Medicaid enrollees to get them to choose their plans.(Some states, though, still allow a person to choose between the regular program and an HMO.) When you get ready to select your plan, ask your state Medicaid office if it has counseling services that can help you pick a plan. You might be able to get counseling in person or over the phone. Some states will also mail you additional materials on the plans to help you make your choice.

Some of these HMOs have been caught offering illegal gifts to get people to join. You should never join a plan because you are offered a gift, money or any free services. In most states, this is illegal, and you should report it to your Medicaid office. Generally, there are a few guidelines you should follow.

• Look for a plan that has your doctor in it. Your doctor will likely not be part of the network of all the HMOs from which you can choose. If your doctor is not in any of the plans, then find out what doctors in the plan are located near your home.

• Choose a plan that has the right mix of services for you. Ask if there are hospitals and pharmacies located near your home, so you will not have transportation problems.

• Take a look at any special needs in your family. Do you or a member of your family have any problems that require special care, such as diabetes or glaucoma? Does the managed care plan have a program for consumers with these problems?

continued

- Find out all you can about the rules of belonging to a Medicaid managed care plan in your state.
  - When can you join, and how long do you have to make your decision?
  - Can you visit plans' and doctors' offices before you join to see if you are comfortable with the surroundings and the people who work there?
  - Can you leave the plan you join if you are unhappy with it and its providers? What do you have to do to leave one plan and join another? How easy is it for you to change doctors within a plan?
  - Will you have to pay any money out-of-pocket (copayment) to see a doctor after you join a managed care plan?
  - What do you do if you have a problem with the plan? How do you complain about how the plan treats you? Is there anyone who can help you file a complaint? In Maryland, for example, every local health department has an **ombudsman**, or troubleshooter, whose job it is to help consumers on Medicaid deal with problems in managed care.

OTHER ASPECTS OF MANAGED CARE

Certain aspects of managed care now play roles even for consumers who belong to traditional indemnity insurance plans. These insurance plans—which are sometimes referred to as **managed indemnity plans**—now nearly always use **utilization review (UR)** for their members. To control costs and, in some cases, to check whether the services prescribed for the member are appropriate and covered by the insurance company's contract, a UR program oversees the services that members get, how frequently these services are used and how much they cost.

UR programs generally look for ways to keep consumers from using expensive services such as hospitals unnecessarily, to keep close tabs on the number of visits that consumers make to doctors and to monitor prescription drug use. They can also include **prior authorization** (getting permission to have a major diagnostic test) and **precertification** (**preapproval** for an admission to the hospital). While UR can reduce some waste, some physicians and consumers think it often creates unnecessary hassles that have little benefit for consumers. For the remainder of this book, we will use the term *managed indemnity plans* to describe indemnity plans with UR.

For many people, joining a managed care plan will provide a much-needed way to coordinate and organize health-care needs. Managed care plans do many things that help many consumers. On the other hand, for many consumers, HMOs impose rules and restrictions on care that are difficult to get used to. In either case, when you join a managed care plan:

- Prepare for changes in how you get your health care.
- Expect to challenge some decisions made by the plan.
- Push your doctor for answers to questions about why he recommends some tests or treatments but not others.
- Take the time to learn how your plan pays doctors in its network.
- Take action against the managed care plan if you do not get the answers you want.

In the next chapter, we take a look at some of the potential advantages and disadvantages of managed care. We also lay the groundwork for helping you select a managed care plan and picking your providers from the plan's network.

2 Understanding the Advantages and Disadvantages of Managed Care

Managed care not only holds promise for helping health-care consumers but also has the potential to help solve some pressing national health-care concerns.

HOW MANAGED CARE CAN IMPROVE ALL HEALTH-CARE DELIVERY

The benefits of managed care fall into seven important areas.

• At least for now, it looks like managed care is helping restrain the overall growth of health-care costs. Health maintenance organizations (HMOs) do this mostly by demanding discounted prices from doctors and hospitals for care. It is not known, however, whether this trend toward lower prices will continue over the long term. HMOs and other managed care plans have not covered enough of the population for a long-enough time for researchers to know whether the slowdown in the growth of health-care costs is due solely to the discounts that managed care plans get from providers or to truly improved management of care.

• Hospitals and physicians are operating more efficiently in order to attract HMOs. In most localities, HMOs sign contracts with only a few of the doctors and hospitals in the area. This forces doctors and hospitals to compete economically in order to be awarded an HMO's business. This forces the providers to lower their own costs and to strive to improve the quality of their care. Doctors are taking steps to reduce overhead costs and the number of unnecessary tests they perform, and they're cutting down on questionable procedures. Hospitals are closing wings, eliminating certain unprofitable services and "closing" beds that are unused because they are costly to maintain.

• HMOs, more so than other kinds of managed care plans, are collecting and analyzing data on how well they deliver care, such as identifying what percentage of children in an HMO are immunized. This information is combined with **outcomes data** (see chapter 4) to help document how well the HMO is meeting its members' needs. Consumers may use this information to help choose an HMO. The HMO industry is working to find ways to report this information to employers who want to offer HMOs to their employees. On the national level, a private organization called the National Committee for Quality Assurance (NCQA) is developing **report cards** and ratings of HMOs and other managed care plans. NCQA is one of three nongovernmental oversight groups that review HMOs and other managed care plans to see how they stack up against performance standards. (See chapter 3 for additional information on performance standards and managed care plan **accreditation**.) NCQA's long-term goal is to create report cards that tell how HMOs perform in a wide variety of services and treatment outcomes.

One problem with NCQA's process is that the data submitted by HMOs and other managed care plans are not audited, or checked, by the NCQA to ensure honesty and accuracy. Hence, some states are developing their own HMO report cards. In fall 1997, Maryland is scheduled to release the first state-government-sponsored managed care report cards in the nation. These report cards will assess all plans licensed to do business in Maryland and will report a wide variety of managed care financial and performance data. In addition, Maryland officials will audit the data that plans operating in Maryland submit to NCQA to ensure that the data are accurate.

• Managed care plans are gathering and analyzing outcomes data for many clinical services. Outcomes data—information that tells how well a patient or a group of patients do when they receive a particular service, such as cataract surgery—go one step beyond service data, such as how many children in a plan were immunized. Outcomes data measure how much of a difference the intervention made in the consumer's health and quality of life. Good outcomes data help doctors, consumers and managed care plans understand if a service is worthwhile.

• Managed care plans are creating **disease management programs** and **care pathways** (medical "road maps" that help plans and physicians determine what services consumers with particular medical problems should receive and from whom). For example, an HMO could design and implement a disease management program for diabetic patients that combines health education, routine blood sugar testing, doctor visits and drug therapy. HMOs develop their disease management programs with the help of experts in particular medical specialties, and they rely heavily on the latest studies of what works best for particular types of patients.

• Plans are continuously studying new medical technologies and drugs in order to keep abreast of new products and services and to determine what is safe and most effective for consumers and under what conditions these services or products should be made available. They are assessing everything from what prescription drugs to offer to what kinds of surgical implants HMO members should be receiving.

• Plans make extensive use of allied health-care professionals such as physician assistants, nurse practitioners and certified **nurse-midwives**. These practitioners, who have less training than physicians, work with doctors to provide many basic health-care services to consumers and are less costly than physicians for HMOs to employ. They can also perform many of the primary care tasks that physicians do and provide very high-quality care for a wide range of illnesses.

ADVANTAGES AND DISADVANTAGES OF MANAGED CARE

Managed care plans such as HMOs have specific advantages and disadvantages when compared with other health insurance options. And even within managed care, HMOs are themselves unique from other managed care options: preferred provider organizations (PPOs), point-of-service (POS) plans and managed indemnity plans. While HMOs, PPOs, POS plans and managed indemnity plans can make it easier and more efficient for you to get high-quality, affordable health care, they also have some shortcomings that might leave you dissatisfied. In this chapter, we will look at the pluses and minuses associated with each of these kinds of managed care.

Among the managed care choices, HMOs are the most re-strictive option. On the other hand, while HMOs have the most rules to follow, they also are more likely to offer more services from a single organization than other managed care plans. PPO and POS plan rules are less restrictive than HMO rules, and managed indemnity plans are less restrictive still. In PPOs, POS plans and managed indemnity plans, instead of relying upon the network of hospitals and physicians assembled by the HMO, you will get all the same services that an HMO provides, but you will need to do more provider shopping on your own.

As managed care options vary in their restrictiveness, so, too, do they vary in a consumer's out-of-pocket expenses. Out-of-pocket expenses come in the form of monthly premiums, deductibles and copayments.

• Your monthly premium is the amount that you pay, often out of your paycheck at work or directly to your insurer from your own pocket, to have health insurance coverage. Your employer may pay part or all of your health insurance premium as a benefit of employment.

• Your deductible is a specific amount of money that you must pay out-of-pocket, directly to health-care providers, each year before your insurance begins to pay any expenses.

• Your copayment is the amount that you pay each time you use a service, such as visiting a doctor in an HMO, PPO or POS plan. In a managed indemnity plan, you will likely pay the entire cost of a doctor visit and wait for the insurer to reimburse you, after you have met the annual deductible.

Your monthly premium will vary depending on the contract between your employer and your HMO, PPO, POS plan or managed indemnity plan. In these four managed care options, HMOs usually have no deductibles and low, if any, copayments, while PPOs and POS plans generally have higher copayments and may have some deductibles for services such as hospitalization. Finally, managed indemnity plans usually have the highest copayments and deductibles (see table on page 46).

However, while out-of-pocket expenses are important, they are only one of the factors to consider when you are deciding whether to enroll in an HMO, PPO or managed indemnity plan. You should also look at which providers have contracts with the plan and what services are covered by the plan.

ADVANTAGES OF HMOs

HMOs offer some powerful advantages over PPOs, POS plans and managed indemnity plans. These advantages operate at two levels. First, there are direct benefits to you, the consumer.

Second, there are potential benefits to the health-care system as a whole that may help improve the quality of health care and help control health-care costs as well.

First, let's take a look at the direct advantages of HMOs for consumers. An important perspective to keep in mind about HMOs is that they are managed care at its most coordinated, most comprehensive level. When developed, organized and well managed, HMOs can provide consumers with high-quality health care that is also economical.

• *One-stop shopping for health care.* HMOs typically offer comprehensive packages of services—everything from physician services to hospital care and access to prescription drugs. This creates a sense of order and structure for health care, which can help you make better sense of what services to get, when and where to get them and from whom. For example, many consumers think it is helpful to not have to look too far to find a

Typical Out-of-Pocket Costs in Managed Care

PLAN TYPE	COPAYMENTS	DEDUCTIBLES	OVERALL OUT-OF-POCKET COSTS
HMO	Very low	Low or none	Very low
PPO	Low	Low or none	Low
POS	Variable	Variable	Moderate
Managed indemnity	High	High	High

specialist. Yet most HMOs give members more than one specialist in each category, requiring the consumer to still ask probing and important questions to choose the best one. Consumers also like having ready access to services such as smoking cessation and stress management classes, programs not often provided in other insurance models. And most HMOs offer their members a full range of services, including physician care, hospital care and even home health care.

• *Coordination of care.* HMOs help their members coordinate their care and get services in the right setting, at the right time, from the right person. This starts with your primary care doctor, whom you will select from a list the HMO gives you when you join. HMOs use primary care physicians (family physicians, internists, pediatricians, and obstetrician/gynecologists) to help direct consumers' health-care needs. They play the role of gatekeeper, or traffic cop, directing you when you need a specialist, specific treatment or diagnostic test. For example, if you have an eye disease such as glaucoma, your primary care provider may set up regular appointments for you with an ophthalmologist and arrange to receive reports, lab results and lists of the drugs you are taking. This is critically important to good health care and can help avoid side effects from adverse drug interactions.

Through the use of computers, HMOs can also coordinate record keeping in such a way that every doctor taking care of you has easy access to your **medical records**. This helps reduce the number of repeat tests and improves communication among your medical providers, all of which is to your benefit.

This kind of management is generally not present in PPOs, POS plans and managed indemnity plans. These three managed care options typically do not require you to select a primary care physician to oversee your care. You can see whom you want when you want, but this greater freedom creates the potential for inefficiencies such as repeat tests and procedures. And these inefficiencies increase not only your risk of complications—tests and procedures all carry some degree of risk or injury—but also your costs, through more copayments and, later, higher premiums.

• *Preventive health care.* HMOs offer their consumers more preventive health-care services and early disease-detection programs. This helps keep costs down and is an important way to help consumers in HMOs maintain a higher quality of life. It is in your—and the HMO's—interest to prevent diseases or catch them early, when they are easier and cheaper to treat. HMOs cover many kinds of screening programs (such as mammograms for women and cholesterol checks for adults over age 40) and preventive medicine programs (such as childhood immunizations and nutrition counseling). Full coverage for preventive medicine and early disease detection is much more spotty among POS plans and PPOs and frequently is completely absent in managed indemnity plans. If because of family history or other factors you are at risk for a certain disease (such as breast cancer or heart disease), or if you have a young child, you would likely benefit from the emphasis on early disease detection and prevention that HMOs offer.

• *Health education and wellness programs.* Aside from the wide variety of health education and wellness programs, many HMOs also produce wellness guides and regular newsletters to help their members take more active roles in their own health care.

• *Low copayments for doctor visits.* Consumers in HMOs generally pay little out of their own pockets when they see a doctor. It is typical for a consumer in an HMO to pay a flat copayment (anywhere from $5 to $15) for an office visit to her primary care doctor or a specialist. Copayments in PPOs, POS plans and managed indemnity plans are usually higher than in HMOs (see page 46). Copayments in PPOs are lower than those in POS plans and managed indemnity plans. In a managed indemnity plan, you usually pay a fixed percentage of the doctor's charges out of your own pocket, and this could be as much as 25 percent of the total cost of the visit. Then you wait to get reimbursed later by the insurance company, if you have met the annual deductible.

• *Low copayments for other health-care services.* In an HMO, if your primary care doctor approves an emergency room visit, lab test or x-ray or admits you to the hospital, your HMO, in most cases, will pay for all the associated costs. You will not need to pay any more money out-of-pocket. Generally, a PPO member also pays very little if she is admitted to the hospital with her doctor's approval. The exception to full payment for hospital care by an HMO or PPO is if you use the emergency room for a problem that your primary care doctor could have cared for. For example, going to the emergency room for a minor sore throat, without a fever or cough, is probably not going to get paid for by the HMO, while a visit for chest pain or a severe cut is (see page 50).

In a managed indemnity plan, you must first meet an annual deductible before coverage begins and then have a copayment that, rather than being a fixed amount, could be as much as 25 percent of the hospital's charges for your care. These days, the utilization review part of a managed indemnity plan may also review your emergency room visit to see whether it was **medically necessary** and to determine who should pay.

• *Access to prescription drugs.* Most HMOs provide consumers with a benefit for prescription drugs (although not all employers choose to offer an HMO's prescription drug benefit). This benefit usually lets consumers get their prescription drugs from the HMO's own pharmacy or from retail pharmacies that have a contract with the HMO for a fixed copayment, usually $5 to $10 per prescription. Increasingly, however, HMOs themselves are not providing this benefit directly. Coverage is likely to be provided by another company called a **pharmacy benefit manager**, or **PBM**. We will talk more about PBMs in chapter 6.

MANAGED CARE AND EMERGENCY ROOM VISITS

Getting your emergency room bill paid by a managed care plan might be a problem if the plan thinks you went to the emergency room for something other than an emergency. A commonly heard complaint about managed care has been from consumers who went to the emergency room with frightening—but, in actuality, not life threatening—symptoms (such as burning chest pain that turned out to be heartburn) and were stuck with the bills when their plan refused to pay. In these cases, the plans based the coverage and payment decision on the diagnosis, which is made after you've been seen and treated.

Of course, hindsight cannot take into consideration the fear and concern that consumers had at the time. When the diagnosis is ultimately something that is not life threatening, many plans believe they should not have to pay for the care. Many plans further reason that the consumer should have sought care from her primary care physician, which is usually less costly.

Health maintenance organizations (HMOs) base these decisions on what is called a reasonable physician standard. In other words, they believe that the average, reasonable physician would not send a consumer to the emergency room for what is anticipated to be a case of heartburn. Obviously, most consumers do not have the medical training to make a diagnosis before seeking medical care, and there are many symptoms that could lead you to seek emergency medical care.

continued

But because of consumer pressure, the rules are changing. Sixteen states have passed reasonable *person* standards for managed care plans to pay for emergency room care. Under these laws, a managed care plan must pay for the emergency room care sought by any consumer whose symptoms would lead the average, reasonable *person* (as opposed to the average, reasonable *physician*) to seek immediate emergency medical attention, without contacting her primary care doctor or the managed care plan first. Several members of Congress have indicated that they intend to introduce federal legislation so that all managed care plan members have the same protection.

This is not to say, however, that you should use an emergency room when you do not need to. Your HMO will provide you with guidelines on what to do in emergencies. These include how to contact your primary care doctor or the HMO's helpline for instructions. Whenever you can, you should try to follow the HMO's guidelines. *But you should never let the guidelines stand in the way of getting the immediate help you or a family member needs when problems arise.*

Prescription drug coverage is less likely to be part of a PPO or a managed indemnity plan, unless your employer decides to add it as a benefit, which most larger employers do. Over 90 percent of consumers who have employer-based health insurance have a prescription drug benefit, although most of these programs are limited coverage either provided as part of the major medical portion of an indemnity plan or provided exclusively when a person is a hospital inpatient.

• *No paperwork or bills in HMOs.* Consumers in HMOs virtually never have to deal with paperwork such as bills from their doctors or **claim forms** from their insurers. When a consumer in an HMO uses a service (as long as she does so according to plan rules), she rarely pays anything other than a copayment. The rest of what is due to the doctor or hospital is paid by the HMO. Any receipts or claim forms that your doctor gives you at the time of a visit are simply for your own records. PPOs and POS plans are similarly free of paperwork. Managed indemnity plans and the indemnity "side" of POS plans, however, can still carry a substantial amount of paperwork—getting bills and claim forms, paying bills yourself and keeping records, filing them and waiting for payments.

CONTROVERSIES SURROUNDING MANAGED CARE

While the managed care industry believes it consistently provides consumers with high-quality, cost-effective medical care, it will be some time before we know the long-term impact of managed care on the health and welfare of consumers.

With the exception of a few plans, most HMOs and other managed care plans have not been in existence long enough to know how well they work when they are responsible for the care of large numbers of consumers with varying degrees of needs. Until the rapid growth of managed care in the late 1980s and early 1990s, few health-care consumers in the United States were in any kind of managed care plan. The consumers who were enrolled tended to be young, employed, middle class and generally healthy. Thus, they were a group of people for whom serious illnesses were relatively uncommon. These people likely benefited from things such as the HMO's emphasis on preventive care, health education and routine checkups. In short, they were the perfect HMO consumers: people who need and use very few services, which results in lower costs for the HMO. These patients allow the HMO to make money since they use fewer services costing less than the premiums the plan collects.

The managed care industry is now attracting a larger, more diverse range of subscribers that will put financial pressure on plans. In particular, HMOs are enrolling increasing numbers of Medicare and Medicaid beneficiaries. These members, by definition, are older or less affluent and in poorer health. So they use more services, which costs plans money. It is not yet clear how well these consumers will do in HMOs or other types of managed care. In fact, one 1996 study of older, chronically ill persons concluded that they do better in traditional indemnity insurance plans than in managed care. While other studies also show that consumers with serious illnesses do not fare as well in managed care as in fee-for-service plans, it is too early to draw any firm conclusions.

Managed care may not continue to hold down health-care spending over the long term, particularly as more medically needy and demanding consumers enroll. It is possible that the cost containment we have seen in the past few years is a short-term phenomenon. Managed care plans have squeezed a lot of excess costs out of the health-care system by driving hard bargains on the fees they pay health-care providers, but they might not be able to continue to extract these savings. There may not be anything left to squeeze out.

The trend toward managed care has not helped reduce the number of Americans who lack health insurance. Most of these consumers are fully employed but are shut out from purchasing insurance because their employers do not provide it or the workers cannot afford the premiums.

The push to design and control health-care services at the corporate level of an insurance company also is potentially damaging to the relationship between consumers and their physicians. Corporate policies designed to save the plan money can reduce the amount of time that a provider devotes to the consumer, which may result in a lack of effective communication between consumer and provider. Plus, financial incentives that HMOs use to pay doctors and hospitals can pit your health-care needs against the financial needs of the doctor or hospital, which can lead to your being denied certain services.

For many consumers, an important part of health care is the emotional and psychological support they get from their practitioners. Consumers want the reassurance that their doctors will serve as their advocates when there are problems with managed care plans. The movement to managed care is changing the level of trust between consumers and their health-care providers. Some physicians in managed care see themselves as employees of the plan rather than professionals. This can lead a doctor to less aggressively defend the needs of individual consumers, out of fear that speaking out too loudly or too frequently could lead the managed care plan to drop her from the plan's network. It also forces a doctor to be loyal to the managed care plan (now her employer) and its financial well-being, as well as to her patient. Of course, this creates a conflict of interest because the physician's legal and ethical responsibility is to you, the consumer, not to a third party like the managed care plan.

Physicians paid on a fee-for-service basis also have a conflict of interest. They derive a direct financial benefit from the tests and procedures they perform. Some physicians make decisions on this basis. For example, several studies show that some cities have higher rates on certain surgical procedures than other cities with similar populations. This means some consumers get unnecessary surgeries, which surgeons have financial incentive to perform.

Another example of conflict of interest occurs when physicians send patients to lab or x-ray facilities they own. Federal and some state laws generally prohibit this kind of activity under certain circumstances. For example, *with certain exceptions,* a physician cannot refer a Medicare or Medicaid patient to a lab or x-ray facility that she owns. If she does so, neither Medicare nor Medicaid will pay for the test or x-ray.

No matter what kind of managed care program you join—HMO, PPO, POS plan or managed indemnity plan—the plan's administration will play an important role in your health care. In managed care, you and your physician are not the only parties who decide what care you can receive. Before the rapid growth of managed care in the 1980s, insurance companies had relatively little control over the decisions of health-care consumers and their doctors, which contributed to skyrocketing costs. In managed care plans, the pendulum swings to the opposite extreme. Plans' tight control over how and where care is provided, who provides it and how it is paid for is relatively new in American health care. Historically, physicians controlled these aspects of health care. The control imposed by managed care is potentially helpful in controlling costs and improving care. There is clear evidence that many consumers receive unnecessary tests and procedures under the fee-for-service system. Control by managed care plans is ultimately harmful, however, if it denies consumers access to appropriate and necessary medical care.

The key decision makers in HMOs and other managed care programs often include not only physicians but also the companies' business executives and other administrators who have no direct responsibility for consumers' medical needs and no medical training. This administrative team often makes key decisions about who provides care and how that care is delivered.

The plan's administrators decide what doctors and hospitals are included in the HMO's or PPO's network and how they are paid. The decision about how to pay health-care providers influences what services you receive because the providers may share the costs of the services you get. Thus, if they give you too many tests or procedures, they could lose money because the plan limits what it will pay them. We discuss the impact of managed care payment mechanisms in chapter 4.

Your access to services beyond your primary care provider, such as specialty care or physical or occupational therapy, may also be constrained. Your managed care plan may limit the number of visits you can make to a specialist or therapist and what drugs you can use. You may need approval from the plan to see a specialist on more than one occasion. While limits such as these can help reduce the use of unnecessary or wasteful services, a managed care plan's decisions in this area frequently are financially driven.

In other words, the limitations are designed to save money rather than defined based on what is medically appropriate for consumers with a particular diagnosis. For example, in July 1996, a large Maryland HMO directed its primary care doctors to limit all their referrals to specialists to one visit per patient per diagnosis, with most follow-up care to be done by the consumer's primary care physician. It sent a letter to the plan's doctors (but not to the plan's members) and told the doctors that the HMO's decision was driven by a large increase in spending on specialty care. The HMO did not support its mandate with evidence of what kinds of visits were most costly. Nor did it provide evidence that the limitation on access to specialists was standard for the managed care industry. After considerable public pressure—after the letter was leaked to the press and the controversy exploded—the HMO clarified its stance on visits to specialists.

Insurers have engaged in cost containment activities for the past 10 years or more. But the growth of managed care has brought it to a new level of intensity, and more consumers than ever are affected. For example, the managed care plan you join may decide in what settings you get certain kinds of care, such as approving what surgical procedures are done on an inpatient or **outpatient** basis. The plan will also try to ensure that consumers who are admitted to the hospital are discharged in what it thinks is a timely manner. Consequently, some managed care plans' limits on hospital stays, for example, are creating controversy. For example, some plans were requiring that mothers and their new-born babies be discharged from the hospital within a day of the child's birth, which many physicians and mothers believed was too soon. Now many managed care plans are subject to both state and federal laws that require them to let the mother and baby stay in the hospital for up to 48 hours after the birth, if the mother and physician decide such a stay is appropriate. There is a similar controversy brewing over whether plans send mastectomy patients home too soon. This issue is still being debated by experts and policy makers.

FOR-PROFIT VERSUS NOT-FOR-PROFIT MANAGED CARE PLANS

One of the key differences between managed care and the traditional indemnity insurance system is the influence of huge, publicly traded for-profit companies such as United HealthCare and Health Net. These for-profit managed care plans have come on the scene relatively recently and are growing rapidly by merging with or buying other, smaller HMOs.

Profit status is one factor that you can consider when you choose among plans. While it is not a major factor, such as whether the plan has a doctor you are comfortable seeing and who is affordable, there are some things you should understand about the differences between for-profit and not-for-profit plans that might influence your thinking. Whether a plan is for-profit or not-for-profit is less important than how much money it actually spends on health care for consumers versus plan administration. The amount of money spent on health care is called the **medical loss ratio**, and is usually expressed as a percentage of all the premium dollars collected by the plan from employers and individual consumers. For example, if a plan has a medical loss ratio of 80 percent, it means that the plan spends 80 percent of all the premiums it collects on health care for plan members.

A plan's administrative expenses include salaries for plan employees, costs for computer systems and such, marketing, advertising and profits to shareholders.

The growth of for-profit companies in managed care has both advantages and disadvantages. For-profit, publicly traded companies (their stock is traded on the New York Stock Exchange and other places) such as United HealthCare and Aetna-US Healthcare have very divided loyalties. Their first and foremost responsibility is not to consumers or health-care providers but to shareholders. Like any for-profit, publicly traded company, if a for-profit managed care company reports lower-than-expected profits, the stock price may drop, and shareholders may become discontented.

There was a dramatic example of this in January 1997, when the stock prices of several large for-profit HMOs fell dramatically. The fall in share prices was in response to news that the federal government might cut the money it pays these HMOs to take care of Medicare beneficiaries who join HMOs. Investors lose confidence that the company will remain a profitable investment, making it difficult for the company to attract new stockholders. Also, every time the stock falls, so might the value of the benefits packages that are provided to many HMO executives. These factors conspire to create immense financial pressure for the management of a for-profit managed care company.

For-profit managed care plans contend that because they sell stock to investors, they can raise money in the stock market to develop new programs and services. They also claim that their profit-driven mentality is critical to controlling costs over the long run because it encourages their managers and the health-care providers with whom they contract to serve consumers as efficiently as possible.

It is too early to tell if the claims of for-profit managed care plans are true. They have not existed long enough for anyone to evaluate whether they are better or worse for consumers over the long run, as we have said before. Despite the lack of evidence to support the claims of for-profit managed care plans, you should recognize that there is also little evidence that says not-for-profit plans are perfect. Most not-for-profit plans, with the exception of certain plans such as Kaiser Permanente, have also not existed long enough for us to know with any certainty whether they serve consumers' needs better than for-profit plans.

Some facts are known, however, that might help you choose between a for-profit HMO and a not-for-profit HMO. For example, consider the following:

• For-profit HMOs generally spend less money than not-for-profit plans on direct medical care for their consumers.

• For-profit HMOs spend more money than not-for-profit HMOs on advertising and marketing.

• For-profit HMOs are more likely than not-for-profit HMOs to pay their executives very large salaries and bonuses. Some chief executives at leading for-profit HMOs earn millions of dollars per year while simultaneously asking consumers and doctors to cut expenses and make sacrifices in the name of creating a better health-care system. In general, chief executives at for-profit HMOs earn more than chief executives at for-profit non-health-care companies that are similar in size.

• For-profit HMOs whose stock is traded on stock exchanges often pay their investors dividends. This, of course, is money that is not going to pay for health care for members of the HMO and is not reinvested in the company to improve the services it provides. Rather, this money is treated as part of the administrative costs of running the plan.

• For-profit HMOs rarely, if ever, make consumers an integral part of how the plans are run. Few for-profit HMOs follow the model of the Group Health Cooperative of Puget Sound, which includes a not-for-profit HMO in the Seattle area. Group Health has a long history of consumer participation in both running the HMO and in identifying and solving problems in the individual centers and clinics where consumers get care.

When you choose among managed care plans, you must know which plans are for-profit and which are not-for-profit. Choosing a not-for-profit plan will not ensure your satisfaction, but it may put you in a plan whose mission and goals are more aligned with your own. In August 1996, *Consumer Reports* reported on a survey of 20,000 consumers who rated their managed care plans. According to this consumer survey, the 11 highest-rated plans were all not-for-profit.

You should recognize, however, that not-for-profit plans, like for-profit plans, make mistakes in managing consumers' care and make decisions that can harm their members. They do this primarily by providing poor-quality care. For example, in April 1997, Kaiser Permanente (a national not-for-profit plan) paid a $1 million fine in Texas to settle allegations in a state insurance department report that criticized the plan's quality of care. When you choose a plan and are trying to differentiate between for-profit and not-for-profit plans, focus on the medical loss ratio—how much the plan actually spends on health care for plan members.

HOW MANAGED CARE AFFECTS THE WAY HEALTH-CARE PROVIDERS WORK

Managed care is undoubtedly changing how health-care providers work. In many areas, managed care is creating fierce competition among health-care providers for managed care plan contracts. Hospitals and doctors are eager to win lucrative contracts from local managed care plans in order to ensure a steady stream of customers. Without the contracts, the providers lose business to the plans and suffer financial losses, potentially even going out of business. The competition is leading to some interesting innovations, as hospitals and doctors try to prove that they are providing less costly and better-quality care than in the past. While some of these innovations began before managed care took hold, their growth has accelerated, along with the growth of managed care.

• Providers are reducing inefficiency and waste in their own operations. For example, some hospitals and doctors do less unnecessary testing before surgery.

• Hospitals are developing care pathways to help move consumers through their hospital stays as efficiently as possible. In a care pathway, the hospital studies the services the patient needs and plans the entire treatment program for the whole stay. For example, if a consumer enters the hospital for knee surgery, the hospital may already have a knee surgery pathway starting with the consumer's admission that addresses all services from surgery to rehabilitation therapy. The care pathways help consumers get consistent care and help caregivers in planning. And while it is not possible to have a care pathway for every diagnosis, most hospitals can benefit from such programs. Pathways also allow for contingencies for unexpected complications or problems.

• Some physicians and hospitals are merging into physician hospital organizations (PHOs) to share the costs of taking care of consumers in HMOs. In PHOs, physicians and hospitals can also share administrative functions such as billing and collecting money from the HMOs, maintaining medical records systems and purchasing supplies. They also stand to lose money if they provide unnecessary tests or procedures to consumers. Conversely, they can make money by providing high-quality care more efficiently.

• Physicians are joining larger groups of doctors that can provide a wide range of primary care and specialty services. This makes it easier to refer consumers from one doctor to another. As with PHOs, forming large groups allows physicians to share the costs of caring for consumers in the HMOs (see page 62).

SHARED FINANCIAL RISK IN MANAGED CARE

Managed care has resulted in health-care providers sharing the financial risk of taking care of consumers. *Financial risk* is a term that applies to the parties in managed care who stand to make or lose money on your care. These include your employer, the managed care plan and, today, your health-care providers. In indemnity insurance plans, the only parties who took financial risk were traditional indemnity insurers and the employers and consumers who paid insurers' premiums. Health-care providers—doctors and hospitals—took no financial risk and were essentially paid for whatever services they performed. They had no incentive to document the value of the services they provided, nor did they have any reason to be cautious about what they did or to limit their use of questionable tests or procedures.

In managed care, doctors and hospitals frequently find themselves in a position to share the costs of the services they provide. An example is capitation, in which a doctor receives a fixed sum each month from the managed care plan to care for a consumer. Out of this payment, the doctor must provide care to the consumer and, potentially, also pay for some tests and referrals to specialists. There are other kinds of managed care arrangements in which providers and managed care plans share risk. For example, health plan administrators can assess how well the doctors perform against criteria such as the number of hospital admissions, tests ordered or referrals to specialists and overall patient satisfaction with care.

continued

The doctors can receive bonuses from the plan at the end of the year if they held down costs for the plan and if patients were satisfied. If costs exceeded expectations or consumers were dissatisfied with services they received, then bonuses could be lower or eliminated altogether. In these and other risk-sharing mechanisms in managed care, doctors and hospitals must weigh the cost implications of their treatment decisions for consumers.

When health-care providers share financial risk with managed care plans, they are less likely to order unnecessary tests or procedures or to use expensive drugs when there are equally effective, lower-cost alternatives available. Unfortunately, it can also mean that some providers deny medically appropriate care to consumers in order to ensure that they do not lose money.

Thus, consumers need to watch risk-sharing arrangements between their providers and their managed care plans. You should ask your doctor whether she shares financial risk with the managed care plan you belong to. If she does, you should also ask that the doctor always provide you with a complete list of your treatment or diagnostic options, regardless of the financial consequences for the doctor.

Recent federal rules will help limit how much money health-care providers who take care of Medicare HMO members can lose in the care of individual consumers. True, the rules formally apply only to Medicare HMOs, but they stand a good chance of becoming standard for the industry. The rules say that a Medicare HMO must tell Medicare beneficiaries who join what level of financial risk the plan shares with its health-care providers.

continued

Also, the rules require doctors to carry additional insurance—called **stop-loss insurance**—to limit the amount of money they can lose on any single Medicare HMO patient to $40,000. This means that if any physicians' group, for example, has a very sick HMO member, once they spend $40,000 on the care of this person, the stop-loss insurance starts paying the bills. This will, hopefully, reduce any doctor's incentive to limit care for a consumer, because of a fear of financial losses.

Now let's take a look at the ins and outs of actually selecting a managed care plan.

3 | *Selecting Your Managed Care Plan*

*U*nfortunately, not all medical consumers have a choice about which managed care plan to join. About half of all American workers who get their health insurance through their employers do not have multiple health insurance options since their employers provide only one health insurance plan. Nowadays, that option is usually some form of managed care—frequently a health maintenance organization (HMO), a preferred provider organization (PPO) or a point-of-service (POS) plan.

But even if you have no choice, keep reading. Here's why: Most employers annually reevaluate the health insurance plans they offer employees. By reading this chapter, you can provide some feedback to your employer on how your company's health plan stacks up against the guidelines we discuss here. If it does not measure up, you might suggest that your employer consider offering another health insurance plan. In addition, even if you have no choice, you should understand the issues in this chapter so that you have a better idea of how health insurance plans work. The information will help you deal with plan problems, make you a better-informed consumer and empower you to get the most from your plan.

Under the following circumstances, you will usually have several plan options from which to choose:

• You work for an employer who offers a health insurance plan as a benefit of employment, and there are two or more plans available. Usually, these employers offer health insurance options to their employees once a year, during a period called **open enrollment**. Open enrollment, which usually occurs during the late summer or fall, is when employees evaluate their health insurance options and pick new plans or return to their current ones for the next year.

• You are self-employed or work for an employer who does not offer health insurance (for example, a small business that cannot afford it), and you want to buy health insurance as an individual. In this case, you will probably choose from a number of health insurance plans in your area that take individual enrollees. You will likely choose from HMOs, PPOs and managed indemnity plans. State laws differ on whether health insurers must accept consumers as individual enrollees and when during the year consumers can join plans. Check with your state insurance department to learn how and when you can join a plan as an individual.

• You are a Medicare beneficiary and live in an area where Medicare HMOs are soliciting enrollees. Medicare HMOs do not have a specific open enrollment period. Medicare enrollees can join or leave an HMO at any time.

• You are on Medicaid, and your state government wants you to go from the traditional Medicaid program into a managed care plan such as an HMO. Depending on where you live, you may choose from one of several HMOs that accept Medicaid enrollees. Each state decides its own timetable for when consumers who are eligible for Medicaid may choose an HMO.

• Your employer offers at least one health insurance option, and your spouse's employer also offers at least one health insurance plan. You need to decide what plan is best for your family.

DEFINING YOUR GOALS

Before choosing among your managed care options, you need to answer four important questions for yourself.

1. **Are you now enrolled in an HMO, PPO, POS plan or managed indemnity plan, and are you satisfied with the services you have received?**

    If you are pleased with your current plan and like your doctor, then you should keep it high on your list of options. But do not shut the door on another plan. If you are unhappy with your current plan, then you need to study your available options to determine if another plan can better meet your needs.

2. **Is your current health insurance plan no longer an option?**

    It is possible that even if you like your current plan, it is no longer an available choice. For example, your plan may have raised its premiums to a point where neither you nor your employer can afford it. Or your employer may have decided to offer a plan that has a different package of services or a different network of providers.

3. **Do you currently have a physician whom you like and trust?**

    This is one of the most important factors in deciding which managed care option to choose. If you like and trust your primary care doctor or a particular specialist and believe it is important to maintain a relationship with him, the plans that have contracted with that doctor should be at the top of your list. If your current doctor is not available under your plan options, then your choice of plans is more problematic. You will then need to evaluate other physicians in addition to the plans themselves. (See chapter 4 for a full discussion on how to choose a doctor in a managed care plan.)

Under these circumstances, you will most likely part company with your current physician. Of course, if the plan is a POS model, you can continue to see him, but you will have to pay a percentage of his fees out of your own pocket.

Sticking with a doctor you know and trust is important, especially if you have a chronic health problem and are happy with your doctor's treatment. Your relationship with your doctor is likely to have a strong overall influence on your satisfaction with the managed care plan. Your doctor is often the key to getting access to services in the plan, including diagnostic tests, specialists and hospital services. He is also your advocate and can help you challenge the plan's management if you have a problem getting access to tests or treatments.

4. **In addition to your physician, do you prefer a particular hospital and want to continue to have access to it?**

This issue is especially important if you have a **chronic illness** or disability and receive care at a hospital that has special services to meet your needs. For example, children with chronic illnesses (such as sickle-cell anemia) often do better at facilities that specialize in those conditions—facilities that have specially trained doctors and nurses and specific counseling programs designed for those patients and their families. A switch to a hospital that lacks those special resources can have potentially disastrous results.

GETTING INFORMATION ON YOUR MANAGED CARE OPTIONS

Unfortunately, much of the information available to rate your managed care options is marketing material supplied by the plans themselves. Each plan wants your business (especially if you are healthy and not likely to incur many costs) and will gladly brag about its virtues. Obviously, no plan will divulge its blemishes and the services it does not perform well.

To effectively evaluate your managed care choices, you will need to coordinate information provided by the plan with what you learn from your employer, friends, family and coworkers. You should also contact the appropriate state regulatory agency (most likely your state health or insurance department) to see what information it has about the managed care plans operating in your state. This should include the number of complaints filed against a managed care plan, the nature of the complaints and their resolution, if any.

Some of your state's regulatory agencies (such as the health department, insurance department and attorney general's office) may have information they can send you on managed care plans in your state. This might include business and financial information the plans file with the agencies, such as changes in membership, information on financial solvency and other background data. However, you must ask the agencies for this information since they do not routinely disclose it to consumers. These state agencies may also be working on HMO report cards. For example, New York, Florida, Minnesota and Maryland, among others, are developing HMO report cards for plans that do business in their states. Maryland is planning to be the first state to produce such a report—its report is scheduled to be released in late 1997.

Your local newspapers and magazines may also produce managed care plan rankings you can use before making your choice. These reports could include information such as consumer satisfaction with local plans, the number of doctors and hospitals affiliated with each plan and data on how many consumers joined or left each plan last year.

Each state has a regulatory agency—usually the insurance or health department—that issues **licenses** to managed care plans that want to do business in the state. Licenses go to plans that meet the requirements set forth in state law. These typically include demonstrating that the plan has adequate money to pay its bills and that the contracts it enters into with employers, health-care providers and consumers are written in accordance with state law. By obtaining a license, the plan agrees to abide by all the state laws that apply to managed care plans. Plans that violate state laws are subject to penalties such as fines or, in worst cases, having their licenses suspended or revoked. Once a license is suspended or revoked, the plan can no longer do business in that state until any problems are fixed and the license is restored. You can find out whether a plan is properly licensed or has had any problems in the past by calling your state insurance or health department.

Informal information sources, such as friends, coworkers, family members and even your doctor, can also provide you with a wealth of information. By asking these people about their experiences with managed care plans in your area, you can get a picture that goes beyond ratings and plan marketing materials. You may also learn how the individual plans you are evaluating treat a wide range of consumers and how well they work with health-care providers to ensure that consumers get the care they need.

MANAGED CARE PLAN ACCREDITATION

Beyond what a few individual states are doing, there is little independent, objective information to help you understand differences among plans. However, improvement is on the horizon. Managed care plans are applying for accreditation with one of three national organizations: the National Committee for Quality Assurance (NCQA), the Joint Commission on Accreditation of Healthcare Organizations (JCAHO) or the American Accreditation Healthcare Commission (AAHC).

Accreditation is a review process in which a managed care plan is measured against a set of specific standards to see how well it is performing. In managed care, accreditation reviews are conducted by one of these three private, nonprofit organizations. After NCQA, JCAHO or AAHC completes its review, it decides whether to accredit the plan. The accreditation, which is typically for one to three years, is the equivalent of a stamp of approval indicating that the managed care plan meets the accrediting group's standards.

Accreditation is a *voluntary* process—in short, managed care plans choose whether to participate. In addition, the plan pays a fee to the accrediting group for the "honor" of undergoing the process of evaluation. Accreditation is not the same as licensure. Most managed care plans are required to apply for licenses from the states in which they operate and do business.

Managed care plans seek accreditation for a number of reasons. Some employers will do business only with accredited plans. A managed care plan that is not accredited is at a competitive disadvantage in its market. On the other hand, it is important to know that NCQA, JCAHO and AAHC have no enforcement authority over the plans they accredit. No matter how badly a managed care plan performs, the accrediting organization cannot close it down or bring civil or criminal penalties against it. Only the state regulatory agency that licenses or regulates the plan can do that.

In order for a managed care plan to maintain accreditation, the accrediting agency may direct the plan to take corrective action to resolve any problems uncovered during a review. If the managed care organization fails to make the correction, the agency can only deny or take away accreditation.

The three accrediting organizations work independently of one another and are, in fact, competitors. Each organization is to some degree an arm of the managed care industry. Their boards or ownership includes representatives from hospitals, physicians' groups, large employers and the insurance industry. Few consumers are on their boards of directors. Even though the accreditation process is a welcome attempt to create reliable and objective information for consumers, no one really knows yet whether accreditation makes a difference in the quality of care. Also, it is not yet known which of the three accrediting bodies does the best job. It will take more years of research and evaluation before this question is answered. However, NCQA is the farthest along of the three in terms of the number of plans it has reviewed.

Let's take a closer look at the three accrediting bodies now.

National Committee for Quality Assurance (NCQA)

NCQA started in 1979 as a joint venture of two managed care industry trade groups—the Group Health Association of America and the American Managed Care and Review Association, which merged to create the American Association of Health Plans (AAHP). AAHP is a trade group that represents the interests of managed care companies, and it plays an important role in NCQA.

NCQA's board of directors has three consumer representatives: one from Consumers Union, the organization that publishes *Consumer Reports;* one from the American Association of Retired Persons; and one from the United Auto Workers. The remaining board members represent health-care providers, managed care plans, consulting companies and major employers or business groups. There are several important things to know about NCQA's accreditation process.

NCQA reviews managed care plans for accreditation in six areas.

- Quality improvement
- Physician credentials

- Members' rights and responsibilities
- Preventive health services
- Utilization management
- Medical records

Where levels of accreditation are concerned, NCQA can make a range of accreditation decisions after its review of a managed care plan.

- Full (three-year) accreditation is granted to plans that meet NCQA's most rigorous standards. As of May 1997, 50 percent of reviewed plans were fully accredited.
- One-year accreditation is granted to plans that do not meet enough quality standards to earn full accreditation. As of May 1997, 34 percent of reviewed plans had one-year accreditation.
- Provisional accreditation is granted for up to one year. Plans provisionally accredited must show progress in quality before moving up the accreditation ladder. As of May 1997, 6 percent of reviewed plans had provisional accreditation.
- Plans are denied accreditation when they do not meet NCQA standards. As of May 1997, 7 percent of reviewed plans were denied accreditation.
- Accreditation is considered under review when NCQA has made an accreditation decision but is reviewing it at a plan's request. In these cases, NCQA and the plan may disagree about NCQA's decision. During the review, NCQA can change its initial decision to give the plan a better accreditation. As of May 1997, 3 percent of plans had their accreditation under review.

NCQA makes reports on managed care plans available to employers and consumers.

Employers can purchase the Health Insurance Employer Data Information Set (HEDIS). HEDIS shows service and outcomes data that managed care plans report to NCQA. NCQA *does not* check this information for accuracy or honesty. Employers who purchase HEDIS reports must decide what information to share with their employees about plans in the area. NCQA is also incorporating HEDIS into a new product called Quality Compass for employers and other large organizations. NCQA will not have a consumer version of HEDIS for some time to come.

Consumers can get two reports: the Accreditation Status List (ASL) and the Accreditation Summary Report (ASR). The ASL shows which managed care plans are accredited and for how long and which ones have been denied accreditation. The ASR is a two-page summary of NCQA's accreditation report on a specific managed care plan, including how the plan ranks in the six quality areas noted previously. Consumers can compare one plan with another and assess each plan against national averages that appear in each report. ASLs are available at no charge by calling 800-839-6487. ASRs (not yet available for all accredited plans) cost $3 each if ordered from the toll-free number above. They are also available free on the Internet (http://www.ncqa.org).

Joint Commission on Accreditation of Healthcare Organizations (JCAHO)

Started in 1951 as the Joint Commission on Accreditation of Hospitals, JCAHO is a not-for-profit joint venture of several medical groups, including the American Medical Association and American Hospital Association. JCAHO has expanded over the years to include accrediting long-term-care facilities, home care organizations (1988) and, most recently, managed care plans. The board of commissioners (equivalent to a board of directors) consists mainly of health-care interest groups such as doctors, dentists and hospitals. The six "public members" include professors of law and business, a labor union representative and an insurance industry representative.

JCAHO accredits managed care plans in eight areas.
• Rights, responsibilities and ethics
• Continuum of care

- Patient education and communication
- Health promotion and disease prevention
- Network leadership
- Human resources management
- Information management
- Performance improvement

Where levels of accreditation are concerned, JCAHO can make a range of accreditation decisions after reviewing a managed care plan, all of which are communicated to consumers through its reports (see below). JCAHO conducts a full review of accredited plans every three years. Between full reviews, JCAHO conducts follow-up assessments of plans in which problems have been identified.

- Accreditation with commendation is the highest form of accreditation, indicating outstanding compliance with JCAHO standards. This level of accreditation carries no additional recommendations for performance improvement.

- Accreditation is granted to plans that are in *acceptable* compliance with JCAHO standards in all areas.

- Accreditation with type I recommendations is granted to plans with at least one recommendation to correct a specific unsatisfactory area.

- Provisional accreditation is granted to plans that comply with some standards but need to improve in other areas.

- Conditional accreditation is granted to plans that do not substantially comply with JCAHO standards and to plans that have specific quality-of-care problems needing rectification.

- Preliminary nonaccreditation is granted to plans that do not comply with JCAHO standards or that have had their accreditation withdrawn for reasons such as submitting false data to JCAHO. A plan can appeal this decision.

- Plans that do not comply with JCAHO standards are not accredited.

Concerning reports available to employers and consumers:

JCAHO offers a list of accredited plans (with level of accreditation) and plans denied accreditation.

You can reach JCAHO at 630-792-5000. JCAHO reports can also be downloaded from the Internet (http://www. jcaho.org).

American Accreditation Healthcare Commission (AAHC)

AAHC was formed in 1990 to set standards for the utilization review industry. Since then, AAHC has expanded its mission to include reviewing and accrediting managed care plans. The board of directors is divided into three groups: managed care industry, health-care providers and the public. Public members include two business groups, one labor union and the National Association of Insurance Commissioners.

AAHC reviews managed care plans in five areas to decide accreditation.

- Participation and management
- Utilization management
- Quality management
- **Credentialing**
- Member participation and protection

Where levels of accreditation are concerned, there are the following:

- Full accreditation is granted for a period of up to two years to plans that meet AAHC standards.
- Provisional accreditation is usually reserved for managed care plans that meet AAHC standards but have been in business one year or less. Plans with this accreditation are revisited six months after provisional accreditation is granted to see if they have progressed enough for full accreditation.
- Plans that do not meet AAHC standards are denied accreditation. AAHC does not tell consumers which plans are denied accreditation.

Reports on managed care plans are available to employers and consumers: Employers and consumers can contact AAHC at 202-296-0120 to get the list of managed care plans that are accredited.

CHOOSING A MANAGED CARE PLAN

Choosing a managed care plan requires answers to a series of important questions. Each question should yield essential information, allowing you to put together a picture of the plan(s) you are considering. Some of the answers may not come easily, but stick to your mission and be persistent. The more you learn about a plan, the easier your choice will be. And the more you know before signing on the dotted line, the more satisfied you will be in the long run.

Here are some questions to help you review your managed care options.

1. Is the plan accredited by NCQA, JCAHO or AAHC?

While it is far from perfect, accreditation shows that the plan is willing to let an independent third party review its operations. By securing accreditation, a plan is also creating a yardstick by which it can be measured against its competitors. *You should not join any managed care plan that, after an accreditation review, is denied accreditation or has its accreditation withdrawn.* Upon additional review by NCQA, JCAHO or AAHC, the accreditation may be granted or restored, which signals that the plan has corrected any deficiencies.

2. Which plan offers the best mix of services to meet your health and medical needs?

Before you start reviewing managed care plans, make a list of your health-care needs. Include all the illnesses for which you or a family member are currently receiving treatment and any prescription drugs or medical equipment that you use. Also, make a list of the doctors and hospitals you would prefer using to compare with those offered by the plan. Also, consider what services you may need in the future. For example, are you anticipating a pregnancy or any kind of elective surgery? By thinking through your specific needs, you can better envision what services and care you will want from your managed care plan and thus choose a plan that appears able to meet your needs.

Chances are that each managed care plan you are assessing will offer a slightly different mix of services. Most plans provide comprehensive coverage for inpatient hospitalization, doctor visits and diagnostic services, such as blood and urine tests and x-rays.

Plans do vary, however, in some service areas. For example, HMOs are more likely than PPOs, POS plans and managed indemnity plans to offer well-baby care, prenatal care and preventive health care such as cancer screenings. Plans also vary in their coverage of vision care (such as routine eye exams, eyeglasses and contact lenses), home care, medical equipment (such as wheelchairs and intravenous pumps to deliver certain medicines), mental health services, substance abuse treatment and rehabilitation services (such as physical or occupational therapy).

The program material you receive from a plan or your employer should provide a brief discussion of what services the plan covers, as well as any limits on the coverage. For example, while a plan may indicate that it covers **mental health care**, it will usually limit the number of days per year for inpatient treatment. It may also limit the number of annual outpatient visits to psychiatrists and other mental health professionals. If you have a specific need that is not addressed in the plan's program materials, check with your employer or the plan.

3. How many and what kind of complaints did consumers file against the plan in the past couple of years? And is the number of complaints increasing or decreasing?

Consumers file complaints against managed care plans for many reasons: problems getting referrals to specialists, **denials of care** (for example, certain tests or treatments), difficulty getting appointments with primary care providers, excessive waiting times at doctors' offices and disputes over billing problems (see page 80). In most states, there are several places where consumers can file complaints about their managed care plans, including the state insurance department, health department and attorney general's office. You should also check with your employer or your union, if you belong to one, to see if any of your coworkers have asked for help resolving problems with the plans offered.

Every managed care plan has a consumer complaint or **grievance** procedure that is typically outlined in membership materials you receive after joining the plan. (It's a good idea to check out this procedure before you join.) If a complaint arises, you will need to follow the plan's appeal or grievance procedure in order to have the problem addressed. (See chapter 7 for a detailed discussion of how to file a complaint against your managed care plan.)

4. If you have a chronic disease (about 100 million Americans do), does the plan have a special program for it?

A managed care plan can take many steps to ensure that consumers with chronic diseases (such as asthma, diabetes, heart disease and high blood pressure) receive care that is specifically targeted to their unique needs. These steps could include letting certain chronically ill consumers use specialists instead of primary care providers to coordinate services with other providers in the plan; giving consumers with chronic illnesses special educational and counseling services to help them cope with their illnesses; and providing con-

CONSUMERS AND HMO BILLING PROBLEMS

In some Maryland and New York health maintenance organizations (HMOs), the members were victims of inappropriate billing practices by doctors and hospitals who were not satisfied with the time it took the HMOs to pay their bills. In these cases, disgruntled providers who were awaiting payment sent bills to consumers for services that the HMOs were obligated to pay. In some cases, the health-care providers also initiated collection proceedings against the consumers, damaging those consumers' credit ratings. In a few instances, the providers tried to garnishee the consumers' wages.

Clearly, this was a sign that the HMOs in question did not have good financial management and lacked either the reserves or the administrative systems to pay their bills on time. In Maryland, the direct consumer billing was a violation of law for both the HMO and the provider. In both instances, the billing violated consumers' contracts with the HMOs.

Ultimately, regulatory agencies in both states intervened to help consumers and saw that the HMOs paid their bills. Maryland's legislature also passed a law penalizing HMOs that do not pay the bills from health-care providers in a timely manner.

sumers access to disease management programs that integrate a large number of clinical, educational and supportive care services into one package.

If you have a chronic illness, call each plan and ask what special programs, if any, it offers for your condition. Then ask the plan to send you brochures or other materials that describe the program.

If the plan does not have materials to share with you, ask to speak with a doctor or nurse who is familiar with the program to get details about the specific diagnostic, therapeutic and educational components of the program. A well-designed disease management program should address all these areas and should not merely be an occasional educational brochure from the plan. You can compare these details across plans and also discuss them with your current physician to help decide what plan to choose.

5. How easy is it for you to change doctors (either primary care doctor or specialists) in a plan?

In PPOs, POS plans and managed indemnity plans, changing physicians is usually not a problem. Typically, you do not have to select a primary care doctor who controls your access to other doctors in the system. In HMOs, however, changing physicians is potentially more of a problem. Ask the HMOs you are considering what limits they place on changing primary care physicians. Can you change whenever you want to, or does the plan decide when and if you can switch? If you need to switch, you should be allowed to select any other primary care provider in the plan's network and not just someone else in the same group as the doctor you wish to leave. Also ask how easily you can change specialists if the first specialist you see does not meet your needs.

6. Can you pick specialists who are not affiliated with your primary care physician's group?

In some managed care plans, when you select your primary care provider, you are also selecting the specific group this doctor belongs to. This could limit your access to specialists in the plan if your primary care doctor is part of a multispecialty group that includes primary care physicians and specialists such as cardiologists and surgeons. The managed care plan may limit you to seeing *only* a specialist who is part of that group.

For each managed care plan you're considering, you should specifically ask whether you can see *any* specialist in the plan's network, even if the specialist you wish to see is not in the same multiphysician group as your primary care doctor.

If a plan limits specialty referrals to only those doctors in the same group as your primary care doctor, you or a family member could get treated by someone who lacks the specific clinical expertise that you need. You could also be forced to end a relationship with a specialist you already see—and like and trust. For example, if your child needs specialized pediatric surgery and the multiphysician group your primary care doctor belongs to does not have a pediatric surgeon, and if you are restricted to using a physician from only that group, you would be forced to use a doctor who typically, say, treats only adults. This could happen even though there are pediatric surgeons elsewhere in the plan's network.

You should avoid managed care plans that limit your access to specialists this way. But if all the plans you are evaluating appear to work this way, you will have some recourse should problems arise. You can appeal special referral limitations to the plan's **medical director** or to regulating agencies such as your state's insurance department.

7. Does each managed care plan you are evaluating have contracts with major local, regional or national medical centers that specialize in certain services?

Some procedures such as complex surgeries and sophisticated diagnostic tests are best performed only at major medical centers. Consumers who need testing or treatment at a major medical center generally have already seen their primary doctors or specialists, who recommended the more sophisticated services that a major medical center can provide. Because you cannot predict when you will need the services of a major medical center, it is important that your managed care plan have contracts with major medical centers in your area or region or, in some cases, elsewhere in the country. These centers are likely to have state-of-the-art diagnostic testing equipment and access to, and knowledge of, the latest therapies.

8. Who in the plan decides what new treatments and tests are covered, and how are these decisions made?

Medical technology is expanding at a very rapid rate. New products and services such as diagnostic tests and drugs come on the scene almost daily. These new products are often expensive and can have an uncertain impact on quality of care. Therefore, in most managed care plans, plan administrators decide what new services to cover in a process called **technology assessment**. Typically responsible for these decisions is the medical director (a doctor in the plan's administration) or committees set up by the plan to assess new technologies.

Plans often have committees that specifically assess new drugs (called **pharmacy and therapeutics committees**) and other committees that assess other services such as new diagnostic tests. Managed care plans are uneven in their approaches to technology assessment. Plans that do a good job of technology assessment thoroughly review medical studies and call doctors in the plan and experts from around the country to help them make their decisions. HMOs appear to offer a more comprehensive approach that includes calling on national experts who are not employed by the plans to help them decide what services to cover. On the other hand, managed indemnity plans are more likely to use an approach in which the medical director, largely on his own, makes a decision to cover a new service—a process that is less thorough and can lead to some denials of necessary care. The bottom line is that it is in your best interest to join a plan that takes a broad view of emerging medical technologies and does not rely heavily on the opinion of one plan official.

9. Will the plan cover and pay for care in a clinical trial?

In some serious illnesses, such as cancer, AIDS and heart disease, you and your physician may conclude that your best treatment option is to receive care in a **clinical trial**. A clinical trial is a study in which doctors assess how well different treatments work in patients with a particular disease. For consumers with a life-threatening illness such as AIDS or some cancers, clinical trials often allow them to be treated with the latest drugs in carefully monitored and controlled circumstances. Treatments provided to consumers in clinical trials are often state-of-the-art therapies and offer the best chance for care or relief of symptoms.

Any managed care plan you join should pay for treatment in a well-run clinical trial that you are eligible for and that is approved by an agency such as the Food and Drug Administration or National Institutes of Health. Managed care plans typically cover care in clinical trials on a case-by-case basis.

10. How are the managed care plans you are evaluating performing financially?

Most managed care plans report their financial performance to a state regulatory agency such as the insurance department or health department. Because most states do not require routine disclosure of this information to consumers, you should call the appropriate agency to find out what percentage of each premium dollar goes to direct medical care.

The amount of money that a managed care plan actually spends to take care of consumers in the plan is the medical loss ratio. The medical loss ratio is essential information because it tells you a lot about the plan's priorities. A good managed care plan should have a medical loss ratio of 80 to 85 percent. In other words, 80 to 85 cents of every premium dollar goes directly to health care. Less money spent on medical care means more money spent on the items listed below.

* *Administration and advertising.* How much does the managed care plan spend to run the plan and advertise it?
* *Profits to shareholders.* A for-profit managed care plan pays profits in the form of dividends or stock splits to the investors who hold stock in the company. A not-for-profit plan does not make these profit payments and can take any money left at the end of the year and reinvest it in the plan for the good of the consumers who get their care from the plan. However, even not-for-profit plans can have low medical loss ratios because they may be lavishing too many benefits, bonuses and salaries on administrators and providers.
* *Executive salaries and bonuses.* How much does the plan pay its executives to run the company? As we noted in the previous chapter, the chief executives of for-profit managed care plans make more money, on average, than

executives at similarly sized companies in other industries. Excessive total compensation packages, in both for-profit and not-for-profit plans, may be a good indication of where the owners' priorities are.

11. **Are any of the managed care plans you are evaluating self-insured plans sponsored by your employer?**

In a **self-insured managed care plan** (and it could be an HMO, PPO, POS plan or managed indemnity plan), your employer is actually paying all the health-care bills, rather than paying a monthly premium to an insurance company, which then contracts with and pays health-care providers. Self-insured plans are regulated by federal law, not by state law, which is how most insurance plans are regulated. Thus, if you join a self-insured plan, you usually cannot get any help with a complaint against the plan from a state agency such as the attorney general's office, insurance department or health department.

The little, if any, oversight of self-insured plans is a problem. They can change benefits at any time, there are few mandated benefits, and there are few laws to make sure the plans stay solvent and can pay their health-care bills (see below).

ERISA

Self-insured plans are governed under a federal law called **ERISA**, which stands for **Employee Retirement Income Security Act**. One of the key parts of ERISA is that it lets federal law take precedence over state law.

continued

If you are considering joining a self-insured managed care plan (you can learn from your employer or the plan administrator whether the pan is self-insured), there are several important things you should know.

• Most self-insured plans use a **third-party administrator (TPA)** to process the claims and sign contracts with doctors and hospitals. The TPA, often a well-known insurance company, generally runs the plan for your employer, pays the claims to providers and often has some authority to decide what services consumers get. Even though your employer pays the bills, the TPA has the right to make decisions on who can get what care and what rules consumers and doctors must follow in association with your employer.

• If you have a problem in a self-insured plan (for example, the TPA denies you coverage for an organ transplant or refuses to pay a bill for a covered service you received from a doctor or hospital affiliated with the plan), you generally cannot get any help fighting this decision from state agencies, which have no jurisdiction over self-insured plans.

Your employer can exert pressure on the TPA to reverse its decision. So when a serious problem arises that your TPA is unable to resolve to your satisfaction, let your boss or your benefits office know. Provide as much detail as possible because you are essentially filing a complaint with your company's benefits office and should follow the guidelines for filing an effective consumer complaint against a managed care plan (see chapter 7). In worst-case situations, you will need to contact a lawyer to consider suing the plan to get what you want.

Finally, ask your employer if the plans you are evaluating are holding informational meetings, either at your workplace or at some other site, to allow consumers to learn more about how the plans operate. Take advantage of these meetings and ask plan representatives the questions outlined here if they are not fully addressed in the materials you get from the plans.

On the following pages is a checklist that summarizes each of these issues. You can use the list to tally and keep track of the different managed care plans you are comparing.

Once you review your managed care plan options, you are ready to start thinking about your choice of physicians. In the next chapter, we will examine how to pick a good doctor in a managed care plan.

MANAGED CARE PLAN EVALUATION CHECKLIST

	PLAN #1	PLAN #2	PLAN #3
PLAN TYPE (check one)	HMO ☐ PPO ☐ IND★ ☐	HMO ☐ PPO ☐ IND★ ☐	HMO ☐ PPO ☐ IND★ ☐
Are you currently a plan member?			
Are you satisfied with current plan? †			
What special medical needs do you have?			
Are your doctor and hospital in this plan?			
Do you want continued access to your doctor and hospital?			

★ IND stands for managed indemnity insurance plan.   *continued*

† Use a scale of 1 to 5 to rate your plan, with 1 being unsatisfied and 5 meaning extremely satisfied.

	PLAN #1	PLAN #2	PLAN #3
PLAN TYPE (check one)	HMO ☐ PPO ☐ IND* ☐	HMO ☐ PPO ☐ IND* ☐	HMO ☐ PPO ☐ IND* ☐
Accredited by NCQA, JCAHO or AAHC? For how long? Accreditation ever denied or withdrawn?			
Complaints filed with the plan and/or a state agency?			
Problems paying bills to health-care providers?			
Special services for chronic illnesses?			
Ease of switching primary care physicians? Ease of switching specialists?			

*IND stands for managed indemnity insurance plan.   *continued*

	PLAN #1	**PLAN #2**	**PLAN #3**
PLAN TYPE (check one)	HMO ☐ PPO ☐ IND* ☐	HMO ☐ PPO ☐ IND* ☐	HMO ☐ PPO ☐ IND* ☐
Access to specialists limited to the group your primary care doctor is in?			
Access to a major medical center?			
Decision process for new technologies?			
Coverage for clinical trials?			
Plan financial data: direct medical care, advertising and administration, profits, executive pay?			

*IND stands for managed indemnity insurance plan.   *continued*

	PLAN #1	PLAN #2	PLAN #3
PLAN TYPE (check one)	HMO ☐ PPO ☐ IND* ☐	HMO ☐ PPO ☐ IND* ☐	HMO ☐ PPO ☐ IND* ☐
Self-insured plan?			
Consumer literature to assist with decision making?			
Plan-sponsored orientation meetings to answer consumer questions and describe plan operations?			
Plan report cards from state agencies, such as health department or insurance department? Plan ratings in each?			
Copayments for primary care services?			

*IND stands for managed indemnity insurance plan.   *continued*

	PLAN #1	PLAN #2	PLAN #3
PLAN TYPE (check one)	HMO ☐ PPO ☐ IND★ ☐	HMO ☐ PPO ☐ IND★ ☐	HMO ☐ PPO ☐ IND★ ☐
Copayments for specialty care or hospitalization?			
Copayments for emergency room care?			
Higher copayment for out-of-plan care?			
Annual deductible before plan begins paying?			
Annual out-of-pocket maximum after which plan pays all expenses?			
Monthly premium for the type of coverage you need (individual, family, etc.)?			

★ IND stands for managed indemnity insurance plan.

4 Picking Your Doctor in Managed Care

Choosing a doctor in managed care requires the same approach as selecting a managed care plan: Know your needs, ask questions, get information from many sources, and be persistent.

Managed care is changing consumers' relationships with their doctors. In most cases, managed care plans have more influence over how doctors interact with and treat their patients compared with traditional indemnity insurance plans. And in some cases, the doctor is a full-time employee of the plan and, therefore, must follow its rules and guidelines. While your doctor's legal and ethical obligation is still to act in your best interest, in today's managed care climate the burden is more on you to ensure that you get the highest level of care possible. You can increase the likelihood of getting high-quality care by knowing your physician's educational credentials and experience, along with her skills. And you should be aware of the pressures that a physician faces in managed care. All these factors have a direct effect on your care and your satisfaction.

If you currently have a physician who participates in a managed care plan you are considering, you should evaluate your relationship with this doctor to decide whether you wish to continue seeing her. Ask yourself these questions.

• How well does your doctor communicate with you? Does she take the time to explain things to you, or does she rush through visits? Are you comfortable speaking with her and confiding in her?

• How well does your doctor run her practice? Is the office a well-organized, friendly environment? Are you treated with courtesy and compassion? Does the staff seem disorganized and have trouble keeping track of patients or records? Do staff members seem to communicate well among themselves, or do they frequently contradict each other when they speak with you?

• Is your doctor readily accessible? Can you reach her directly by phone, or does she rarely return your phone calls? Can you get an appointment quickly in an emergency? What is the typical waiting time to get an appointment for a routine office visit?

• How satisfied are you with your doctor's management of your health problems? Has she been effective in treating your acute problems (brief, sudden illnesses or injuries and the like)? If you have a chronic illness, such as high blood pressure or diabetes, has the treatment been useful? Has your doctor monitored your ailments closely, educated you about your illnesses and referred you to a specialist when it was necessary?

• Has your doctor shared useful educational material with you, such as diet and exercise ideas, weight-loss strategies, smoking cessation plans and contraception information? Has she provided you with written or other materials to help you manage any chronic conditions you have? Has she instructed you in self-care techniques that may help your ailments?

• When you have seen specialists, did your primary care doctor help you choose them? Were you satisfied with her recommendation? Did your primary care doctor follow up with you *and* the specialist to ensure that you received the best care and that you understood the implications of the specialist's recommendations?

• If you had a problem with your insurance company that required your doctor's help to resolve, how effective was the doctor's intervention? Was she willing to support you, and how helpful was her input in getting the problem resolved? For example, did she write letters and make phone calls on your behalf?

• Has your doctor been candid with you about matters such as fees, the cost of recommended tests or treatments and your responsibility for copayments?

If your answers to these questions are generally positive, then consider sticking with your current physician. This is usually easy if your current doctor is a member of the network in the health maintenance organization (HMO) or preferred provider organization (PPO) that you are considering. If you are leaning toward a point-of-service (POS) plan or managed indemnity plan, you can also continue to see your current physician—although you will likely pay more out-of-pocket than an HMO or PPO member would.

So if you choose a managed indemnity plan, or if you use the indemnity "side" of a POS plan, check with the insurer to determine what percentage of your doctor's fees it will pay. In these plans, the insurer pays part of the doctor's fee for the covered services, and you are responsible for the balance. If you join a managed indemnity or POS plan, ask your doctor if she will accept the insurer's percentage of payment as full payment. In other words, negotiate. It is a perfectly legal and normal occurrence in health-care transactions.

If your answers to the above questions are negative or inconclusive, then you need to reevaluate your relationship with your doctor and think seriously about selecting a new one. Choosing a doctor is a multistep process that requires gathering objective information (for example, "Is this doctor certified in any specialty?"), subjective information (for example, "Does this doctor get high or low marks from friends or family members?") and making a personal judgment ("Can I relate to this person and communicate with her?").

UNDERSTANDING THE RELATIONSHIP BETWEEN DOCTORS AND MANAGED CARE PLANS

When you evaluate your choice of physicians in managed care, you should be aware of many important issues concerning their relationships with the managed care plan. Historically, physicians and other health-care providers have not openly and honestly divulged how insurers and managed care plans pay them for care. Consequently, consumers have not realized that payment methods may influence doctors' treatment approaches. Studies show, however, that payment arrangements between physicians and health plans *do* influence care. Thus, it is important to find out just what their business relationships are and to consider how that might affect you and your family.

When you address the following issues with your primary care or specialty physician, you will learn about how managed care plans and physicians interact—if your physician is forthright and honest in her response. You will also learn a great deal about your physician. Not all physicians want to address these complex issues. But you should seek a doctor who does. You can address each of these questions to either your primary care physician or a specialist.

1. "How are you paid by *my* managed care plan?"

As we have noted previously, managed care plans pay physicians in many different ways: capitation, fee-for-service, **discounted fee-for-service**, and **fee schedules** (see page 99). Ask your physician to describe how she is paid to care for you under your plan.

HOW MANAGED CARE PAYS PHYSICIANS

Here are brief descriptions of the most common ways managed care plans pay physicians.

• *Capitation.* Your physician receives a fixed monthly payment from your managed care plan to provide care for you. If you use few services, your physician gets to keep the money that she receives from the plan. If you use a large number of services (such as requiring many tests or procedures), your physician stands to lose money because she must pay for this care.

• *Fee-for-service.* Your managed care plan pays your physician after she provides care to you. The plan pays for each test, procedure or evaluation that the physician provides. The exact amount paid by the plan depends on the physician's fee, as well as on what the plan believes is appropriate. This is the way most consumers are used to having their physicians care for them.

• *Discounted fee-for-service.* This is similar to fee-for-service, except that your physician agrees to take less money than she would in the fee-for-service arrangement described previously. Essentially, your doctor agrees to give the managed care plan a discount from her normal fee and accept a lower amount as payment in full.

• *Fee schedule.* A physician who is paid according to a fee schedule is paid a fixed, predetermined sum of money, depending on the services she provides. The managed care plan makes the payment after you receive your care, so this is a variation on fee-for-service. Physicians who are paid on a fee-for-service basis generally agree to accept the fee schedule amount as payment in full. In most cases, you will have a copayment in addition to what the managed care plan pays.

2. "If your form of payment from my managed care plan is capitation, are you responsible for paying the costs of referrals to specialists, lab tests or x-rays out of your own pocket?"

This commonly occurs in managed care plans that pay physicians using capitation. By sharing financial risk with the physician, the managed care plan is trying to ensure that the doctor makes referrals to specialists or orders tests and x-rays only when *absolutely* necessary. In theory, a physician who is "at risk" for these costs will make more efficient referral decisions. Unfortunately, this is also an opportunity for an unscrupulous physician to deny *appropriate and necessary* referrals or tests in order to keep money in her own pocket.

If your primary care doctor or specialist is paid according to a capitation arrangement, ask whether she has purchased stop-loss insurance that will help cover the costs of a consumer's care once the doctor's spending exceeds a specified amount. For example, in Medicare HMOs, both individual physicians and physicians' groups that care for Medicare enrollees on a capitated basis must have stop-loss insurance. This insurance limits the physician's potential losses on any one Medicare beneficiary to $40,000. While non-Medicare managed care plans are not required to do this, some experts think this will become a standard practice for the way that all managed care plans use capitation.

3. "Do you get an annual bonus or share of profits from my managed care plan?"

Paying physicians an annual bonus is a common practice in managed care. Typically, a physician or the group she belongs to receives a bonus based on how her practice compares with other practices in the plan. Plans look to see how many referrals the physicians make, how many patients they hospitalize, how many lab tests they order and other financial measures. The plans award the best bonuses to physicians or groups whose practice profits are in line with those of others in the plans. Physicians who order higher numbers of tests and procedures may be penalized with lower bonuses, as might physicians who appear to order few tests and procedures, potentially a sign of providing too little care. In allocation of bonuses, the plans also take into account surveys of patient satisfaction concerning specific doctors or groups. Ask your doctor to describe the basis for bonuses paid to her by your managed care plan.

4. **"If my plan denies a treatment or referral that you recommend, how will you work with me to resolve the issue?"**

Managed care plans, doctors and consumers sometimes disagree over physician referrals and/or treatment decisions. Ideally, when such a dispute arises, you and your doctor should demonstrate to the plan that the services recommended are medically appropriate and that there are no other reasonable alternatives. This may require your physician to contact the plan's medical director to discuss the issue, to send the plan letters on your behalf (with studies and data that support this position) and, if necessary, to meet with plan officials. It is critical that your physician be willing to serve as your advocate in disagreements with the plan.

5. **"How does my managed care plan monitor your practice?"**

Most managed care plans try to monitor physicians through a process called **practice profiling**. In this, a plan gathers basic clinical and financial information about a physician's practice and compares it with other practices in the plan, as well as with the plan's estimates of how the physician should be doing. The plan shares these data with physicians in the plan on a periodic basis to let physicians know how they are doing compared with their peers.

This information is used, for example, to help the plan decide whether to renew or terminate contracts with physicians, how much the plan will pay in bonuses and how to change its capitation payments to doctors. If a managed care plan concludes that your physician's practice is inconsistent with the plan's expectations, your physician may have to change the way she cares for patients. This could include making fewer referrals, ordering fewer tests or spending less time with some patients. On the other hand, it could improve your care as the comparative education your doctor receives makes her more efficient.

6. **"How does your office maintain my medical records?"**

Your medical records are private documents that no one should have access to without your knowledge and consent. Some physicians and managed care plans put medical records on computers that are accessible to physicians and other personnel. One computer company is even discussing sharing consumers' medical records among physicians in a plan over the Internet. If your doctor uses a computer to store medical records, or if she shares records with other doctors across computer networks such as the Internet, ask what security measures the office takes to prevent unauthorized access and whether she is legally required to get your consent before doing so. You should also find out whether your doctor will send any information about your medical care, typically by computer, to any kind of outcomes databases.

GETTING STARTED

Most of us start our search for a physician with the selection of a primary care doctor. If you join an HMO or PPO, you will have to select a primary care doctor who serves as your gatekeeper, or coordinator of your care. If you join a POS plan or managed indemnity plan, you will not be required to choose a primary care physician, but you may wish to consider doing so.

A primary care doctor can provide you with many essential services. Unless you have a problem requiring a specialist's skills, your primary care doctor can meet most of your health-care needs and answer a wide range of health-care questions. She can help you decide when to see a specialist and assist you in finding the right one. She can also provide guidance when you need diagnostic tests or other services. A primary care doctor is important because of the relationship you build with one another. As a result, the doctor understands your overall health-care needs and becomes your partner in managing them. In that same vein, she monitors the care and services you receive from the various specialists you may see.

When choosing a primary care doctor, you will generally select one of the following types of physicians:

• **Family physicians.** These are doctors who care for children and adults of all ages. Family physicians provide a wide range of general medical care, including some obstetric and gynecologic care, as well as perform minor surgical procedures such as suturing wounds.

• **Internists.** These physicians are trained in adult internal medicine. They typically provide less pediatric, obstetric and gynecologic care than family physicians. They may, however, consult with family physicians or other primary care doctors on specific problems, and they frequently have special expertise in an area of internal medicine such as cardiology.

• **General practitioners.** These are physicians who, like family physicians, care for a wide variety of ailments. While fewer and fewer medical students choose to become general practitioners, a number of general practitioners still practice.

• **Pediatricians.** These physicians are trained to take care of children, from birth through roughly age 20. In many managed care plans, if you have children you can select a pediatrician as their primary care doctor and another physician (such as an internist) to meet your own needs.

• **Obstetrician/gynecologists.** These doctors are trained in women's health, including prenatal care and labor and delivery. Some managed care plans let women choose obstetrician/gynecologists as their primary care providers. Other plans require women to get referrals from their internists or family physicians to see obstetrician/gynecologists.

• **Geriatricians or gerontologists.** These doctors specialize in the medical care of older consumers. If you are an older consumer who is joining a Medicare HMO, for example, you may wish to choose a geriatrician or gerontologist as your primary care provider, if your HMO has one available. As the population ages, and more Medicare enrollees join HMOs, gerontologists will increasingly be an option.

CHOOSING A PRIMARY CARE DOCTOR

When you review your options for a primary care doctor or specialist (see page 114 for more information on choosing a specialist), you will need to rank your health-care needs and then find the doctor who you think is best equipped to meet them. Use these questions to guide your search.

1. **What are your health-care needs, and what do you expect from your primary care doctor?**
   Your search for a physician starts with you and your needs, not with the list of physicians provided to you by your managed care plan. Start by listing the qualities you want in a doctor. Also list your ongoing medical needs. Add to this any other factors that are important to you (for example, evening or weekend office hours).

HOW MANAGED CARE
PLANS CHECK OUT DOCTORS

A managed care plan uses a process called credentialing to evaluate physicians before letting them join the plan's network. The National Committee for Quality Assurance requires that a plan being reviewed for accreditation demonstrate that it has a thorough credentialing process. The plan's credentialing process must examine each physician's background for evidence of fraud, criminal activity, disciplinary actions and **malpractice** history.

While this is an admirable standard, remember that not all managed care plans are accredited, nor have they all asked to be accredited, so not all credentialing processes are as good as they could be. And even if a plan examines a doctor's background, it may still elect to sign up a doctor with a questionable record. Sometimes this is the only doctor in the area with a specialty that the managed care plan needs to include in its network in order to be competitive.

Some managed care plan executives even admit that their credentialing processes leave much to be desired. In the August 1996 issue of *Consumer Reports,* Michael Stocker, M.D., president of Empire Blue Cross and Blue Shield, one of the largest plans in New York, admitted that plan "credentialing is not a very good screen... almost totally useless."

The credentialing process does not guarantee that a doctor who is a member of a health maintenance organization (HMO), preferred provider organization (PPO) or point-of-service (POS) plan network is necessarily

continued

better than one who is not. Being a member of a managed care plan network may indicate nothing more than the fact that the doctor passed basic checks of her qualifications and agreed to care for consumers at the plan's fees, while similarly qualified—or even better-qualified—physicians refused to accept the plan's fees. You also cannot assume that all the physicians in a plan are equally well qualified to care for you.

Despite what the managed care plan may learn about physicians during the credentialing process, the plan provides limited information to consumers about the qualifications of doctors it contracts. Physician information varies from plan to plan, which means it is hard to compare the doctors in one plan with the doctors in another. For example, one plan may provide brief biographies of its doctors (more common in staff model and group model HMOs with relatively small staffs), while another may provide only a name, address and phone number (more common in larger plans that contract with many physicians).

Because the quality of information on physicians in managed care plans is inconsistent, you need to dig deeper than the information provided to you by the plan. By doing so, you will increase the likelihood of finding a doctor with whom you can build a strong relationship.

2. **What cultural factors are important to you that may help enhance communication with your doctor?**

Consider whether there are any cultural factors that are important to you. For example, if you are African-American, is it important that you have an African-American physician?

Other factors you may wish to consider are language—are you comfortable with English or are you fluent in another language such as Spanish?—and the age and gender of the physician. Because you will likely share very personal information with your primary care doctor, it is essential that you choose the kind of person who is sympathetic to your needs and respects you as a person.

3. **Is the doctor licensed in your state, and has her license ever been suspended or revoked?**

While it does not often happen, doctors do lose their licenses for a variety of reasons, including providing negligent care and assaulting or defrauding their patients. The easiest way to check out the status of a physician's license is to call your state **medical licensing board**. Ask whether the doctor's license is current, whether her license has ever been suspended or revoked, why it was suspended or revoked and whether the license was reinstated. The agency can also tell you if the doctor was ever reprimanded (which is less severe than a license suspension or revocation). Finally, ask the board to tell you where your potential doctor went to medical school, where she completed residency training and whether the agency knows if the doctor is **board certified**. Board certification is evidence that the physician has completed specific training requirements (see question 4 below).

Other resources you can use to check your potential physician's background are the following:

- The American Medical Association (AMA) offers a list of 650,000 physicians in the United States (this includes physicians who do not belong to the AMA), which you can access for free by computer (Internet address: http://www.ama-assn.org). Look for the Physician Select page. If you do not have a computer, you may find the *American Medical Association Directory of Physicians in the U.S.* in your local library. The information in this resource includes where the doctor went to medical school, where she did her residency training (if done) and whether she is board certified.

- Medi-Net is a California company that purports to have a database of all the doctors in the United States. Medi-Net says their database includes all the information in the AMA's records, as well as disciplinary information from each state's licensing board. Medi-Net's information is not free, however. It costs $15 for a report on one doctor and $5 for each subsequent doctor. You can reach Medi-Net toll free at 888-275-6344.

4. Is the doctor you are considering board certified?

Today, primary care doctors complete medical school and then, in most cases, a three-year training period called a residency in their chosen fields, such as family practice or internal medicine. Residency is an apprenticeship where the physician works closely with experienced, licensed and board-certified physicians to evaluate and care for patients in a wide variety of settings. After a doctor finishes her residency and passes a test of her competency, she can identify herself as board certified. While it is not by itself a guarantee of competency, you should look for a physician who is board certified. Board-certified physicians have chosen to continue their education and maintain their credentials. Some managed care plans contract only with physicians who are board certified or **board eligible** to take the board exam.

You can verify board certification by contacting the plan, calling the physician's office directly or calling the American Board of Medical Specialties at 800-776-2378 (for M.D.'s) or the American Osteopathic Association at 800-621-1773, ext. 7445 (for D.O.'s).

Some physicians prominently display their memberships in professional associations as evidence of their competency. Being a member of a group, no matter how official and impressive it sounds, is not evidence of professional competency and is not equivalent to board certification in one of the specialties recognized by the American Board of Medical Specialties. Some physician organizations have nothing to do with professional competency and serve only to protect the financial and regulatory interests of physicians. For example, membership in the American Medical Association or a state medical society is not the same as being board certified. Do not be fooled by membership in organizations—look for board certification.

5. Does the physician you are evaluating still have a contract with the plan, and is she accepting new patients?

The physician lists of managed care plans change over time, and some of the changes are not communicated to consumers. Physicians drop out of the plan, the plan terminates contracts with others, and some of the doctors move, retire or die. The Physician Payment Review Commission, a congressional advisory panel, found that the average turnover rate for doctors on HMOs' lists is 4 percent per year. The American Association of Health Plans found that in 10 percent of managed care plans, the roster of physicians changes by at least 10 percent each year.

To verify your doctor's contractual status with a managed care plan, take these two steps.

- Call the plan to verify that the physician is still with the plan and is accepting new patients.
- Verify the plan's information by calling the office of each physician you are considering.

SPECIALTY BOARDS

One measure of a physician's training and skills is whether she is board certified. There are 24 specialities recognized by the American Board of Medical Specialties (ABMS), a private, nonprofit organization that oversees the quality of residency training programs and the administration of board certification exams by specialty organizations. The 24 specialty areas in which a physician can be board certified are allergy and immunology, anesthesiology, colon and rectal surgery, dermatology, emergency medicine, family practice, internal medicine, medical genetics, neurological surgery, nuclear medicine, obstetrics and gynecology, ophthalmology, orthopedic surgery, otolaryngology, pathology, pediatrics, physical medicine and rehabilitation, plastic surgery, preventive medicine, psychiatry and neurology, radiology, surgery, thoracic surgery and urology.

In addition to board certification in the 24 recognized areas, there are many **subspecialty certifications** that a physician can earn. For example, within internal medicine, there are subspecialty certifications in fields as diverse as adolescent medicine and critical care medicine. If you are unsure about the specialty or subspecialty in which your physician claims board certification, call the ABMS at 800-776-2378 to check whether it is a specialty or subspecialty the organization recognizes.

6. Is the doctor you are evaluating a member of a group that might limit your access to specialists outside the group?

In some managed care plans, when you select a primary care physician, you may also be choosing all the members of that physician's group practice as your providers. This is potentially a problem if you want to see a specialist other than the one who is in partnership with the primary care doctor.

Before choosing your primary care physician, call her office and ask whether she can refer you to any specialist in the plan's network or just to specialists who are members of her group. If she can refer you to someone outside her group, ask if there is a higher copayment to go outside her group.

7. Are the office hours and location of the doctor you are considering convenient?

Is the office close to your home or workplace? Are the office hours convenient? What kind of coverage does the doctor provide during nights and weekends? If you are considering a doctor who has more than one office, ask both your plan and the doctor whether you can visit her at any location or whether you are restricted to one location, except in emergencies.

8. At what hospitals does the doctor have privileges?

Physicians can admit patients only to hospitals that have granted them privileges to do so. Thus, even if your health plan lists a dozen hospitals in its network, your doctor will likely admit patients to only a couple of them, if that many. Make sure the hospitals that your potential doctor admits to are the ones you want to use. If you have an illness that required treatment at a particular hospital in the past, make sure the doctor has **admitting privileges** there—assuming you want to go back.

Once you know what hospitals your potential doctor admits to, you can contact each hospital and find out whether the doctor was ever suspended or reprimanded by the hospital. If she was, ask why (although the hospital may not answer your question) and find out when the suspension ended or what steps were taken to avoid the problem recurring. If the hospital refuses to answer your inquiry, you should check with your state's medical licensing board to see if it has a record of any hospital discipline of the physician you are interested in.

9. Has the physician been sued for malpractice?

This is notoriously difficult information for a consumer to uncover, and the medical profession has been loath to share it with consumers. The National Practitioner Data Bank contains malpractice information on physicians, dentists, podiatrists and other health-care professionals. However, consumers are denied access to that information. The information is available only to hospitals and managed care plans that are credentialing doctors and to certain lawyers involved in malpractice suits against doctors.

Ask each physician you are evaluating whether she has ever been sued and what the outcome of the suit was. If a physician refuses to discuss her malpractice history with you, you should move on to another doctor. You can also check with the courts in the jurisdiction where the doctor practices (or has practiced) to see if any suits, judgments or settlements have ever been filed against the doctor. (Bear in mind that this may be a difficult and time-consuming process. Not every court clerk is willing to assist consumers.)

There is some hope on the horizon that consumers who want this information will eventually be able to get it. The state of Massachusetts has started a toll-free hotline (800-377-0550 for callers in Massachusetts) for consumers to get two-page profiles of physicians licensed in that state.

The profiles contain malpractice information as well as disciplinary history, educational background and other useful information. Consumers can get up to 10 physician profiles per call, free of charge. The database will eventually be available on the Internet. Hopefully, this effort will set an example that other states follow, so all consumers will have easy access to the key information necessary to select a doctor.

10. Does the doctor own or have any financial interest in laboratory, x-ray or other facilities to which she may refer you?

Any physician who stands to gain financially from a treatment decision made on your behalf should disclose this information without hesitation. In many states, physicians are bound by law to disclose their ownership interests to consumers before sending consumers to the facilities. And as we already mentioned, the Medicare program has made it illegal for a physician to own a facility to which she refers a Medicare patient. There are exceptions to this prohibition, however. Group practices are allowed to own certain kinds of facilities, and physicians are generally allowed to maintain small in-office labs for certain types of basic diagnostic tests.

11. Does the doctor you are considering teach medical students or residents at a local hospital or medical school?

Physicians who spend some of their time teaching medical students or residents are often better informed about the latest trends in medicine. Many physicians do this on a part-time basis.

12. Is the physician amenable to a "get-acquainted," or interview, appointment?

Many physicians welcome potential new patients to their offices for a brief visit and a look at the practice. At the very least, the physician should agree to speak with you on the telephone to answer some of the questions raised here before you make a final selection. Avoid physicians who discourage this kind of open interaction or who tell you they will not spend time with you until you select their practice as your primary care provider. You should not have to wait to meet a physician or her staff until after you make your choice.

During this interview, ask the questions that are most important to your needs.

13. What are the doctor's views on matters of great importance to you?

You should ask the physician to tell you her position on contraception, abortion rights and physician-assisted suicide, if these issues are important to you. You might also want to raise concerns such as care for dying patients, heroics at the end of life or more mundane matters, such as the use of vitamin and mineral supplements, if you feel strongly about these matters. You have a right to know where your healthcare provider stands on these types of issues because one day you may need this person to help you through one or more of them.

CHOOSING A SPECIALIST

Choosing a specialist starts with the same process as choosing a primary care physician. First, you must assess your need for specialty care. If you are currently under the care of a specialist, ask yourself the same questions we outlined earlier about your satisfaction with your primary care doctor (see page 104). If you are generally pleased and wish to continue to see this specialist, you will need to ensure that she is available to you through your managed care plan. Call both the managed care plan and the physician's office to verify that the specialist is in the plan's network. Because managed care plans vary in how tightly they control access to specialists, you may or may not need a referral from your primary care doctor to keep seeing your specialist. Check this out with your plan, your primary care provider and the specialist.

If you develop a problem requiring specialty care after you enroll in a plan, or if you need or want to replace your current specialist with another one, the first thing you should do is discuss this with your primary care doctor. Your primary care doctor can help you identify specialists. In an HMO, your primary care doctor's referral options will be limited by the number of specialists under contract to the plan. In a PPO, you will likely have a wider range of specialists from which to choose because the number of specialists in a PPO network is usually larger than in an HMO. In a POS plan or managed indemnity plan, you can likely see any specialist you choose. The plan will pay a percentage of the costs.

To select a specialist, you need to find out the same important basic information you researched in your selection of a primary care doctor: licensure status, board certification, hospital admitting privileges and malpractice or disciplinary history. You also need to get more detailed data that are specific to the particular problem you need help with.

1. What kind of specialty training does the doctor have, and where did she receive it?

Most specialists in the United States were trained at major medical centers, such as teaching hospitals, or hospitals affiliated with medical schools.

2. Is the physician board certified in a particular specialty?

To become a specialist, a physician goes through considerable advanced training beyond medical school and serves a residency of three or more years in the specialty field. Following their residencies, some physicians undertake an additional period of training called a fellowship, which lets the physician develop greater expertise in a specific area. For example, a physician who completes a residency in infectious diseases may do fellowship training in AIDS to complete her education. Then, following residency or fellowship, the physician takes an exam to be board certified in a specialty field.

Be sure to find out if the doctor is board certified in the specific area for which you are being treated. In other words, a board-certified internist is not the same as a board-certified cardiologist (heart specialist). In the latter case, typically the doctor has specialized in internal medicine, then gone on to subspecialize in cardiology.

3. How experienced is the specialist you are considering with your particular symptom or diagnosis?

How many cases has she treated, or how much of a particular kind of surgery has she done in the past two to three years? In medicine, like in many other pursuits, practice and experience improve skill levels. Physicians who see and treat a problem frequently are more likely to catch subtle **signs** of disease that may elude a primary care physician or a less experienced specialist. Likewise, the more surgical procedures a surgeon performs, the better she is likely to perform it. You should evaluate any specialist's experience from three perspectives.

- How many consumers does the doctor see each year with the same symptoms or diagnosis you have, and what percentage of her practice time is devoted to those consumers?
- How long has the physician treated consumers with your symptoms or diagnosis?
- Does the physician participate in teaching or research, such as clinical trials devoted to others with your diagnosis?

When you need the services of a specialist, you should look for someone who has treated a large number of people with diagnoses similar to yours. It may also be helpful to have a physician who teaches medical students or residents or who participates in research activities. This is an asset if your problem is complex or unusual. It also helps ensure that she is aware of the latest medical developments that could help you.

Specialists who perform invasive procedures deserve an additional level of scrutiny. These include surgeons, interventional cardiologists (who perform invasive heart tests such as angiograms) and ophthalmologists (who not only treat eye diseases medically and prescribe corrective lenses but also perform surgery such as cataract extractions). If you need the help of such a specialist, find out how frequently she performs the procedure you are considering and what kind of outcomes information she can share with you (see page 118). Look for a specialist who performs the procedure often and has successfully handled the range of complications that can arise as a result of any surgical procedure.

4. If your specialist is a surgeon, how long have she and her surgical team worked together?

For a surgical procedure such as coronary bypass surgery, joint replacement or a transplant, you must count not only on the surgeon but also on the nurses and technicians who make up the total care team. The longer a team has worked together, the more likely they are to be able to competently handle the complications and problems that occur during major surgery. Look for a surgical and treatment team that has trained and worked together for several years.

OUTCOMES DATA

Outcomes data measure whether a person's health status improves after a particular treatment or procedure or whether the person suffered complications as a result of the care provided. Outcomes data also help you understand how previous patients fared under this doctor's care. Where do you go for this information?

Some states such as Pennsylvania and New York gather and publicly report outcomes data on certain procedures. Consumers can call the state health department to see if there is outcomes information available to help them choose qualified specialists.

Unfortunately, publicly available outcomes data are scant. However, there is a growing trend to increase the availability of such data. Many medical specialty organizations are developing detailed outcomes databases designed to gather and analyze physician-specific information on commonly performed surgical procedures. While this information is intended for use primarily by doctors and managed care plans, you should ask the specialist you are considering if she contributes information to an outcomes database and whether she will share it with you. A competent specialist should be willing to share her outcomes record with you. Walk away from anyone who will not.

5. How will your specialist and primary care provider coordinate your care?

In managed care, specialists do not usually care for patients for a lengthy period of time. Your specialist will do what needs to be done, then release you to the care of your primary care physician. While under a specialist's care, however, you should be told the expected length of her treatment and how she plans to provide updates to your primary care provider on your progress. For example, postsurgery, the surgeon typically provides several follow-up visits. Then after several days, assuming there are no complications, she will refer you to the primary care provider. She should already have sent a summary of the surgery and postsurgical progress (including a recommended postsurgical treatment plan) to your primary care doctor. If you believe that you need additional attention from the specialist beyond what your managed care plan typically authorizes, you should work with both your specialist and your primary care physician to get authorization for additional visits. And in some cases, if you are dissatisfied with your plan's decision in this regard, you may want to appeal the plan's decision.

6. **If you have a chronic condition that requires ongoing specialty care, can you consult a specialist without having to see your primary care doctor?**

As we noted earlier, there is controversy about how well chronically ill consumers fare in managed care. One option you should discuss with your managed care plan is the possibility of using a specialist on an ongoing basis without seeing the primary care doctor. (And frankly, the policies of managed care plans vary as to whether consumers can bypass primary care physicians altogether and see specialists in such situations.)

For example, a consumer with end-stage renal disease (an irreversible form of kidney failure) may do better being under the full-time care of a nephrologist (kidney specialist) than being bounced back and forth between that specialist and a primary care physician. Studies show that specialists such as cardiologists do a better job of diagnosing and treating certain conditions related to their specialties than do primary care physicians.

MAKING THE TRANSITION
TO A NEW DOCTOR

There is a good chance that you will switch to a new primary care physician or specialist when you join a managed care plan—again, though, depending upon the particular type of managed care plan. Here are some tips to help make the transition go smoothly.

• When you are ready to switch physicians, make sure that the physician you are leaving has the name, address and phone number of your new physician. Ask your current physician to forward your medical records, including copies of test results and any x-rays in her possession, to your new doctor. You may also wish to ask for a copy of the records for yourself. Whenever you go to a new doctor, it is always in your best interest for the physician to have a detailed understanding of your medical history—and in the best interest of the partnership for you to know what is in your own medical records.

• Make sure your new physician has a complete list of all the medications that you take, including their dosages. Drug reactions often occur when two or more incompatible drugs are prescribed. You can minimize the risk of such a mistake by ensuring that your new physician knows what you are already taking. Your pharmacy can help you prepare this list, as can the doctor you are leaving. If necessary, when you make your first visit to a new doctor, take all your medicines with you, and let your new physician enter the drugs and their dosages into your medical records.

• Provide your new physician with a list of all the doctors you have seen in the past several years and the reasons you saw them. In the event that a problem resurfaces, for example, your new physician is then better equipped to contact doctors who previously treated you. This list is especially important if you are not able to supply your new physician with copies of your medical records.

CHECKLIST FOR EVALUATION AND SELECTION OF PHYSICIANS

List your health-care needs from and expectations of a physician to help you evaluate your choice of physicians.

	DOCTOR #1 Primary care? ☐ Specialist? ☐	DOCTOR #2 Primary care? ☐ Specialist? ☐	DOCTOR #3 Primary care? ☐ Specialist? ☐
Managed care plan affiliations?			
Licensed?			
Board certification?			
Practice specialty?			
Accepting new patients?			
Convenience factors (hours, locations)?			
Malpractice history?			
Disciplinary history?			
Hospital admitting privileges? Which hospitals?			

continued

	DOCTOR #1 Primary care? ☐ Specialist? ☐	DOCTOR #2 Primary care? ☐ Specialist? ☐	DOCTOR #3 Primary care? ☐ Specialist? ☐
Teaching appointments at hospitals or medical schools?			
Any financial interest in referral facilities?			
Willing to meet with you at no charge to "get acquainted"?			
Position on important issues such as abortion?			
Experience with your specific diagnosis?			
Length of time associated with surgical team?			
How paid by managed care plan?			

continued

	DOCTOR #1 Primary care? ☐ Specialist?　☐	**DOCTOR #2** Primary care? ☐ Specialist?　☐	**DOCTOR #3** Primary care? ☐ Specialist?　☐
Stop-loss insurance for capitated arrangements?			
Annual bonus or profit sharing with plan?			
Physician's financial risk for referrals, tests, etc.?			
Communication with consumers over plan profiling?			
Office medical records system?			
Approach to consumer advocacy in disputes with plan?			

5 | *Getting the Most From Managed Care*

*E*valuating and choosing a plan and doctor is only the beginning of your journey through managed care. Once enrolled in a plan, you need to learn its features, in detail, to get the maximum benefit from it. This requires working with your primary care and specialist physicians, as well as continuing to ask plenty of questions.

Getting the most from managed care requires becoming familiar with the plan's general rules and procedures and learning how to access and use its health-care services. You will need to learn what to do in specific situations, such as emergencies.

THE BASICS

When you enroll in a managed care plan—be it a health maintenance organization (HMO), preferred provider organization (PPO), point-of-service (POS) plan or managed indemnity plan—you will have to deal with some immediate operational matters that set the stage for your relationship with the plan. Here are the important ones.

1. **Membership card.** This is one of the first items you will receive from the plan after it processes your enrollment application. Examine your membership card to be sure that your name and identification number (which is frequently your Social Security number) are correct. Many plans also print your primary care doctor's name—if you have chosen one—on the card. If the primary care physician's name does appear, make sure that the plan has accurately recorded it.

Your membership card also includes important information about how to use some of the plan's services. This information may include important phone numbers, which you should take the time to become familiar with. Usually, you will find the phone numbers for the following services:

- *Emergency hotline.* Many managed care plans now contract with phone-answering services to help consumers who believe they have medical emergencies. (See page 140 for more information on how to deal with medical emergencies in managed care.) Plans' rules on using emergency hotlines vary. Some plans require you (or a family member) to call the hotline before seeking **emergency care.** Others want emergency room staff to call the number when you arrive at the hospital to inform the plan of your situation. If your card does not adequately explain how to use the emergency hotline, look for additional information in your enrollment materials or call your plan's **customer service** hotline.

- *Customer service phone number.* Virtually every plan has a number you can call to ask general questions about plan procedures, to determine whether a specific service is covered, to identify where to go for certain services (such as a lab test or x-ray), to get a referral to a specialist from the plan or to file a grievance or appeal. (See chapter 7 for more information on how to file a grievance or appeal.)

If you ever lose your card, call your plan immediately to report the loss and get a new card. By informing the plan of the loss of the card, you can prevent its fraudulent use, which can cost you and the plan money.

- *Your primary care physician's phone number.* While not necessarily on all plans' cards, this is an essential contact number for you to know. Your primary care physician is the person from whom you will receive most of your health care. He is also your gatekeeper, the person who will help you gain access to many other services in the plan, such as a specialist.

2. **Plan membership materials.** Once you enroll in a plan, you should receive additional information from the plan about specific procedures and plan features. These materials are often called your **evidence of coverage** and should include detailed explanations of what medical and surgical services are covered, what steps to take in specific situations (such as how to get emergency care), what to do if you need care when you are away from home and how (or if) children living away from home (for example, attending college or living with a custodial parent) can get needed care.

Some plans also distribute biographical sketches of physicians who work with them. Some managed care plans, particularly HMOs, provide their members with some basic health and wellness information addressing issues such as diet, exercise and injury prevention. These prevention and wellness materials may also describe the health education programs the plan offers.

3. **Services provided by other vendors.** Many employers provide their employees with vision, dental, mental health and prescription drug coverage from companies other than the managed care plans. Often such firms specialize in these specific services and also provide them at a lower cost to you

and your employer. When this is the case, the services provided by the outside firms are said to be **carve outs** (see page 129). In some cases, your managed care plan and the company providing the carve-out service coordinate their work. In other cases, they work quite independently of one another. Generally, you do not have any choice about what companies will provide the carve-out services; it is a decision your employer makes. Usually, when you select and enroll in a managed care plan, you will automatically be enrolled in the carve-out programs. However, some employers make carve-out services optional, allowing the employee to reduce his share of the monthly health insurance premium.

One of the challenges you'll face in managed care is matching your specific needs to the unique set of services your managed care plan offers.

Most consumers use their health plans to meet a variety of needs; therefore, one savvy way to learn how to use your managed care plan is to look at some common areas in which you and your managed care plan might interact. This will help you understand the key features of managed care plans, the ins and outs of using certain services and how to address questions and issues that frequently arise.

In the following sections, we examine some of the benefits, features and pitfalls of managed care. Let's start where managed care usually delivers at its best: preventive health care.

MANAGED CARE AND PREVENTIVE HEALTH CARE

Ideally, preventive care, or wellness, is where managed care can do you the most good. As we have already noted, managed care plans tend to take disease prevention and wellness more seriously than traditional indemnity insurance plans. Regardless

MANAGED CARE CARVE OUTS

Carve outs are an effort by employers to purchase certain health-care services at a lower cost than even the traditional managed care plans can provide. The companies that provide the carve-out services are also managed care companies, but only for specific services. They maintain their own networks of providers and their own rules about how services are utilized. So in other words, you need to familiarize yourself with these companies as with your actual managed care plan. Here are the typical services provided by such companies.

• *Prescription drugs.* Most consumers in managed care plans have coverage for prescription drugs. While many health maintenance organizations have their own prescription drug plans, this benefit is increasingly provided by separate companies called pharmacy benefit managers (PBMs). The PBM, in concert with your employer, decides what drugs it will pay for and what your copayment for each prescription will be. The PBM also has a network of pharmacies that you can use to get your prescriptions and usually offers a mail-order program through which you can purchase medications. (See page 155 for more information.)

• *Mental health benefits.* Companies that manage mental health benefits take a similar approach. They sign up a network of mental health care providers (including clinical social workers, psychiatrists and psychologists), contract with facilities for inpatient mental health care and establish the rules for how these services are used. (See page 151 for more information on managed care and mental health.)

continued

• *Vision and dental care.* In both of these services, the companies set up their own networks of providers (such as dentists, ophthalmologists, **optometrists** and **opticians**). They also set benefits limits—for example, the plan may cover only two routine dental exams and teeth cleanings per year. The carve-out vision or dental services also usually have their own schedules of copayments and deductibles.

If your employer offers these benefits, each of the carve-out companies will usually send you its own membership card and enrollment materials. Review these as closely as you do your other managed care plan materials.

of your age, sex or health status, you should investigate the range of wellness and preventive health activities offered by your plan. Find the ones that suit your needs and sign up for them.

While each managed care plan covers a wide range of wellness and prevention activities, most HMOs, PPOs and POS plans offer a core group of services. Managed indemnity plans may also cover some of these wellness and prevention activities, but the scope of their programs is typically not as comprehensive. And they are likely to have higher copayments and deductibles attached to them. By making use of the wellness and prevention services that managed care plans offer, you improve your chances of staying healthy. You also increase your chances of discovering problems earlier, when they are more treatable and less costly to manage.

Exactly which preventive services your plan offers depends on the contract between your employer and your plan, as well as state and federal laws, which may require plans to cover some specific services. If you are in a self-insured managed care plan, which is not subject to state law, then your plan is not required to offer preventive health services mandated by your state's laws, such as mammography screening. Self-insured managed care plans subject to ERISA (the Employee Retirement Income Security Act) are required to offer very few mandated health benefits. (See chapters 3 and 7 for more information on ERISA.) Check with your plan to find out whether it is self-insured and whether it is subject to any mandated benefits requirements.

Here are some important wellness and prevention services to look for.

• *Well-baby and well-child visits.* Managed care plans generally provide full coverage for well-baby and **well-child** visits up to young adulthood. Plans typically specify an age in the late teens or early twenties as the point where they stop covering well-child care. These visits help ensure that babies and young children get all their appropriate immunizations, and they help family physicians and pediatricians monitor children's overall mental and physical development.

• *Periodic general physical exams for adults.* Many managed care plans cover periodic complete physical exams—for example, every two years—for adults. The exam, typically provided by a primary care doctor, should include a complete medical history and physical, along with some basic, age-appropriate tests such as blood work and urinalysis. Some people have complete physical exams soon after joining managed care plans in order to establish a baseline of medical information.

• *Gynecologic care.* Most managed care plans cover a woman's annual visit to a gynecologist, which will likely include a Pap smear and other age-appropriate tests. Women who join managed care plans might consider having complete gynecologic exams and discussions with their gynecologists about issues such as contraception (see page 132). Some managed care plans allow women to choose gynecologists as their primary care physicians. Other plans allow visits to gynecologists without referrals from the plans or other primary care physicians.

CONTRACEPTION
IN MANAGED CARE

Coverage for contraception varies from one managed care plan to another. Not all plans cover all potential contraceptive options for a woman. The service most likely to be covered by the widest range of plans is surgical contraception, such as tubal ligation for women and vasectomy for men.

Coverage for other forms of contraception is less predictable. If you join a managed care plan and have prescription drug coverage, you will probably have coverage for oral contraceptives (birth control pills), with the same copayment as for all other prescription medications. Your prescription drug plan may, however, provide you with only a limited number of choices among brands of oral contraceptives. You should look into this if you use a certain brand not covered by your plan. In this situation, you and your gynecologist should work together to assess whether you can safely and effectively substitute a product from the plan's **formulary** or whether you should negotiate coverage of the drug you need with the plan.

For other forms of contraception, such as injectable drugs (Depo-Provera) and implantable products such as Norplant, each plan makes its own decision about whether it covers the product. Often these contraceptives are not covered because they require a visit to the doctor's office for administration, which raises the cost to the plan.

Plans may cover a visit to a gynecologist for fitting a device such as a diaphragm, but they may not cover the

continued

cost of the diaphragm itself or the contraceptive gel used with it. Plans typically do not cover condoms or contraceptive foams, gels or suppositories. If you need one of these products, you will pay for it out of your own pocket. Review your plan enrollment materials and discuss contraception coverage with your physician.

Coverage is also affected by state law. If you are in a plan that is not self-insured—and, as such, is subject to your state's laws—your state government may require the plan to cover contraception as a mandated health insurance benefit. You can check whether contraception coverage is required in your state by calling your plan or your state insurance department.

• *Screening tests.* HMOs, PPOs and POS plans are more likely than managed indemnity plans to cover certain kinds of **screening tests**, such as mammography to detect breast cancer. These tests are typically covered by plans using guidelines such as those developed by the American Cancer Society, National Institutes of Health and other major health groups. Plans cover the tests for consumers who meet the guideline criteria, which can include age and other risk factors for a particular disease. Other common screening tests include cholesterol screening; screening for colon and rectal cancer, prostate cancer, glaucoma and cataracts in adults; and screening for scoliosis and sickle-cell anemia in children.

• *Health education.* Managed care plans that take their mission seriously provide a wide range of health education programs and materials. Services often range from publications and classes to counseling in areas such as smoking cessation, weight loss and stress management. Some plans also conduct periodic health fairs at which consumers can get basic health education materials, enroll in classes and ask questions of plan representatives. Before you join a plan-sponsored health education activity, you might want to ask the plan how it measures the effect of its health education initiatives. After all, if the plan offers a smoking cessation program but cannot tell you how many plan members actually quit smoking and stay smoke-free, neither you nor your plan can make an informed decision about a program's value.

MANAGED CARE AND ACUTE ILLNESS

Unfortunately, for most of us, no matter how conscientious we are about prevention, **acute illnesses** and injuries do happen. Managed care plans are generally well equipped to deal with health-care needs in such situations.

An acute illness is one that occurs suddenly and that is generally limited in its duration, but not necessarily in its severity or impact on your health. Acute illness can range from infections to heart attacks, strains, sprains and broken bones. Regardless of the exact problem, the goal of managing any acute illness is to provide appropriate testing, treatment, follow-up and education as soon as possible (and to prevent any long-term complications). Managed care plans, like most other resources in our health-care system, are usually well designed to primarily address the needs of those with acute illnesses.

When you have nonemergency symptoms that you believe require attention, the first thing you should do is contact your primary care physician for an appointment. In most cases, you will speak with a nurse or another office staff person, who will conduct a brief phone interview to help determine how quickly you need to be seen. Be clear and concise when you describe your symptoms. Always mention the following serious symptoms first, if they are present: fever, difficulty breathing, bleeding, severe pain and any dizziness, loss of consciousness or disorientation. These symptoms will signal the severity of the problem to your physician or his staff and will help them recommend appropriate care. They may direct you to the hospital emergency room or ask you to come in to the office.

If you go into your primary care physician's office, he will evaluate your condition and recommend tests and/or treatments to pursue. Make sure you understand his recommendations and the reasons behind each. Also, ask about the risks and benefits of the tests or treatments he thinks are necessary. You might also want to ask him if he can supply you with any educational materials that will help you manage your illness more effectively after you leave his office, thus minimizing the need for follow-up visits and allowing you to provide self-care at home.

Some acute illnesses require attention from a specialist in addition to a primary care physician. An oft-heard consumer frustration with managed care is the inability to get a timely referral to a specialist from a primary care provider. If you believe that you need to see a specialist, raise the issue directly with your primary care physician and, if possible, obtain his approval for a visit to a specialist before you leave his office.

In the event that he thinks a visit to a specialist is unnecessary, ask him to clearly document his reasons in your medical records and note that he did not make a referral for you. You should ask the doctor whether his decision not to refer you to a specialist affects his financial compensation, either because he would have to pay for the referral out of his own pocket or because your plan monitors how many referrals he makes and could reduce his compensation (see chapter 4 for more information on these practices).

Even though your primary care doctor will not provide you with a referral to a specialist, you might still be able to see one without a referral. Some managed care plans are relaxing their control over consumers' access to specialists. These plans now let consumers call the plans' offices, rather than their primary care physicians, when they believe they need to see specialists, and the plans routinely provide referrals to specialists. Others let consumers see their chosen specialists at any time, but there is a price for this freedom. Specialist visits typically carry higher copayments than do visits to primary care providers.

Nevertheless, the fact is that sometimes your request for a referral to a specialist will be denied, either by your primary care physician or by the plan. In either case, you can appeal the denial through the plan's grievance and appeal process, which all plans have. If the plan denies your request or your primary care physician's referral recommendation, either you or your doctor can appeal the plan's decision. In most cases, you and your doctor will need to work together to resolve the issue. If your primary care physician refuses to make a referral that you think is necessary, you should file a grievance with the plan to secure the referral. (See chapter 7 for more information on plan grievances and appeals.)

If you suffer from an acute illness that is not resolved by working with your primary care physician and specialist, you may need ongoing care for this problem. In this case, the illness is then considered chronic, and, in managed care, this raises a different set of issues.

MANAGED CARE AND CHRONIC ILLNESS

A chronic illness is one that is lengthy in duration (in some cases, a lifelong problem) and requires consistent monitoring and care, by both you and your physicians. Chronic illnesses include diabetes, high blood pressure, arthritis, asthma and heart disease.

If you have a chronic condition, you, your primary care physician and your specialist should coordinate diagnostic testing, medications and possible hospitalization or surgical procedures. You should also seek health education and self-care instruction to ensure that your illness is well controlled and has a minimal impact on your quality of life.

If you have a chronic illness, you face a more difficult challenge in a managed care plan than does someone who uses his managed care plan intermittently for preventive services or acute illnesses. As we noted in chapters 2 and 3, researchers and policy makers are concerned about how well some managed care plans care for consumers with chronic illnesses.

If you have a chronic condition and can keep seeing your current physician through your managed care plan, you might want to consider not changing course, assuming you are satisfied with the current situation. By continuing to see the same health-care practitioner and working with him to identify additional services within your plan, you can ensure continuity of your care and possibly enhance your care. For example, your physician might help you select educational programs in the plan that could improve your health status, minimize complications associated with your illness or provide guidance on self-care (such as at-home monitoring of your symptoms or self-administration of injectable drugs), which can help reduce trips to the physician.

Some managed care plans have excellent disease management programs designed specifically for chronic conditions. These are especially common for asthma, diabetes and heart disease. Check with your managed care plan to see what disease management programs it offers. Successful examples of these programs have proven to be more effective than the care that a single physician can offer.

You should discuss with your physician whether your plan has any restrictions on care—such as a limit on the number of visits you can make to a specialist each year—that interfere with the proper treatment of your condition. If there are limits, ask your primary care physician to outline how you and he can manage your illness within the restrictions. And again, do not be afraid to appeal any restrictions to the plan's management.

If you develop a chronic illness after enrolling in a managed care plan, or if you enroll in a plan and need to find a new doctor to care for an existing illness, you should consider a more activist approach. As with an acute condition, the first step is to meet with your primary care doctor and discuss your diagnosis and treatment options in detail. This should include reviewing current or potential future treatments such as medications, surgery and even counseling. This information exchange with your primary care physician allows the two of you to start setting up a care plan for the future.

Another issue to settle is whether your primary care doctor is the right person to manage your chronic illness or whether you need a specialist. You and your primary care provider may agree that he should manage your illness and that you should seek help from a specialist only if specific problems arise. But before you agree to this course of action, ask your primary care doctor to tell you how many patients with your diagnosis he has cared for and to outline his general approach to your care. He should also explain under what circumstances he seeks the advice of a specialist. A good physician recognizes his limitations and seeks assistance from a specialist when the specialist's expertise is needed, regardless of the cost to himself or the managed care plan.

Both you and your primary care physician must be comfortable with his proposed approach to your illness. If your primary care doctor presses you to let him manage your chronic illness but you are uncomfortable with his strategy, you might want to consider switching primary care providers or seeing a specialist without going through your primary care provider, if your plan allows you to do so. Ask your plan's management to assist in either situation.

Your primary care physician should be able to tell you whether there are any financial constraints in the plan or in the way he is paid that will inhibit your ability to see a specialist at any given time. Ask your primary care physician if he is paid through a capitation arrangement that requires him to pay for a portion of the costs of your visits to specialists (see chapter 4). This happens most often in HMOs but is not necessarily standard practice in managed care plans. If he is not paid through capitation and, therefore, is not directly at risk for paying a specialist's fees, find out whether the plan could potentially penalize him in other ways, such as reducing his annual bonus, which is sometimes calculated on how few referrals a primary care doctor makes.

If you and your physician decide that you ought to be seen by a specialist, ask him for some recommendations from the plan's list of specialists. These may include physicians in the same group as your primary care doctor, as well as other doctors contracted with or employed by your plan. Before you see a specialist, you should check with your plan and the specialist's office to see if there are any restrictions on the number of visits you can make to the specialist. Consider asking the following questions: Is there a limit on the actual number of visits? Do you need a referral from either your primary care physician or from the plan each time you need or want to see the specialist? Must you get a new referral after a certain number of visits (often two or three) in order to keep seeing the specialist? Are you required to pay any additional copayments and deductibles for specialty care?

Also, check with the plan to find out whether the copayments vary if you see someone who works in the same group as your primary care practitioner. Sometimes if such payments are required, the copayments are lower, or waived entirely, for doctors in the same group that your primary care physician is in.

MANAGED CARE AND EMERGENCIES

Managed care plans vary in how they deal with emergency medical care. Most plans have very clear instructions in their literature about what to do in an emergency. Many have even printed key details on their membership cards. The most restrictive plans, such as HMOs, usually require you to follow a set process for obtaining emergency care. The least restrictive plans, such as managed indemnity plans, impose fewer rules up front, when you need care. But they review emergency care after it is delivered (through utilization review) to ensure that the plan ultimately pays only for emergency care that was truly medically necessary.

If you belong to an HMO and face a medical emergency, prepare to follow certain steps.

• If at all possible, first try to contact your primary care physician, who can either arrange to see you right away or authorize you to go to the nearest emergency room.

• If you cannot reach your primary care physician, your plan may have a separate phone number for you to call in emergencies. This number, which you will find in your membership materials and/or on your membership card, typically connects you with an emergency hotline. The hotline is usually staffed by nurses or other health-care professionals who are trained to assess your situation over the phone. *When you call the hotline, it is essential for you to state as clearly and calmly as possible the most serious symptoms that you or your family member is having. These might include fever, difficulty breathing, chest pain, severe abdominal pain, bleeding or loss of consciousness.* The hotline staff uses a system called **triage**, which helps the staff rank patients according to their symptoms—who should be tended to ahead of others. The hotline staff relies on a combination of computer programs and judgment to decide the appropriate course of care. They are supposed to direct seriously ill consumers to a facility for immediate medical care (see page 141).

• If you cannot reach your primary care physician or the hotline, or if you are away from home when a problem occurs, get medical help as soon as possible. After the immediate crisis

GETTING APPROPRIATE EMERGENCY MEDICAL CARE

While it is important for you to try to follow the rules for emergency care established by your health maintenance organization (HMO), you should never jeopardize your or a family member's health to do so. Despite their best efforts through emergency care hotlines and triage systems, HMOs make mistakes when deciding how to care for some consumers who have symptoms requiring emergency care. In some cases, consumers who should be referred to emergency rooms are not, or they are sent to distant medical facilities in the HMOs' networks, rather than the closest emergency rooms. Either of these errors can lead to tragic consequences because care is unnecessarily delayed.

If the emergency hotline your HMO operates does not provide you with satisfactory assistance and the symptoms persist, get medical attention immediately. When you arrive at the emergency room, have an emergency room physician contact your HMO to report your illness, and when you are discharged from the hospital, make sure you get a copy of your medical records. You will need this if your HMO refuses to pay for the emergency room care. If your HMO does refuse to pay for the care, you can challenge the HMO about whether it is responsible or not. (See chapter 7 for details on how to respond to your HMO if it refuses to pay a bill.)

passes, you or the medical provider who treated you should contact your HMO to report what happened. This usually improves the likelihood that your HMO will approve payment for any care you receive.

If you belong to a PPO, POS plan or managed indemnity plan, you may not have to follow such rigid rules. In these plans, use of emergency services is usually examined after the fact through utilization review. Utilization reviewers, typically nurses or claims assessors, may ask to see your medical records in order to justify paying an emergency room bill. If the health plan believes that you made an unnecessary visit to the emergency room, it could deny payment, leaving you to bear the costs. While this was common a few years ago, it is less so now. Pressure from consumers, employers, physicians and political leaders have awakened managed care plans to the difficulty a consumer has determining what is and is not an emergency.

Because of these utilization review checks on emergency room bills (the costs of which are generally high compared with similar services in physicians' offices), it is wise for you to visit an emergency room only if it is absolutely necessary.

MANAGED CARE AND HOSPITAL SERVICES

All managed care plans cover hospital services for their enrollees. They do not, however, cover services at all hospitals. Managed care plans selectively contract with hospitals in their areas and offer their members access to facilities that the plans believe offer high-quality care at the best prices.

Your choice of hospitals in managed care (particularly HMOs, PPOs and POS plans) is more limited than in managed indemnity plans because they typically have fewer facilities in their networks. Your choice of hospital is further limited by factors having to do with your primary care physician.

• You need your doctor's approval to be admitted to the hospital. Your physician must be able to document for the plan that hospitalization is necessary and that equally effective care cannot be provided on an outpatient basis. Because many managed care plans measure physician performance in part by the number of consumers admitted to the hospital each year, your physician will not admit you to the hospital unless it is essential. In fact, this may be to your advantage, given the hazards of unnecessary hospital stays to a person's overall health.

• Your doctor will probably have admitting privileges at several hospitals affiliated with your managed care plan. This means that if you need hospital care, you may be admitted to one of those. If you wish to be admitted to another hospital in the plan, or to one not in the plan, you may need to either have your primary care physician refer you to another doctor or ask the plan to have you admitted through another doctor.

• If you require a particular hospital service such as coronary bypass surgery, your managed care plan will usually have a contract with specific facilities to which it refers most such patients. When you are admitted to the hospital, it will probably not be by your primary care physician but instead by the surgeon or other specialist who is in charge of your care. If your managed care plan limits you to a specific hospital for a highly specialized service, you should ask about the experience and success of the hospital in treating consumers with your diagnosis. For example, how many cases were treated at the hospital in the past three years, and how well did those patients do after their treatment?

Ask for the **mortality** (death) **rates** for the procedure. Ask, too, for the **morbidity** (complication) **rates** for the procedure. Plans often have this information—make sure you get it. This information is called outcomes data. With it, you might want to compare information from one hospital with information from others in your area. Also, contact your state health department to see if it collects and disseminates outcomes data on hospitals, such as information for certain surgeries. For example, in New York, the state health department collects and makes available to consumers information on how each hospital's open heart surgery program compares with others. If the hospital your plan uses does not compare favorably with other hospitals, you should ask your physician whether your surgery can be performed at another facility.

Unfortunately, some managed care plans choose hospitals more because of price than because of quality-of-care measures. When this happens, a managed care plan may contract with a cheaper hospital even when a clearly superior facility is also interested in affiliating with the plan. You should resist your managed care plan's designation of a hospital for a major surgical procedure if you have any questions about the quality of care provided at the facility. Work with your physician to challenge the plan's decision on where you should have your surgery.

PREMATURE HOSPITAL DISCHARGE

No one should ever stay in the hospital a minute longer than is absolutely necessary. On the other hand, your managed care plan should not push you out the door before you are medically ready. In recent years, managed care plans have garnered negative publicity and a flurry of state and federal legislation aimed at preventing early hospital discharges, allegedly brought on by health maintenance organization policies. One such controversy centered around the release of mothers and their newborn children from hospitals less than 24 hours after labor and delivery. This led to state and federal laws

continued

aimed at preventing **premature hospital discharges**. Another controversy centers on same-day mastectomies, but Congress and state legislatures appear to be moving more slowly here.

Remember that when you are hospitalized, the only person who can authorize your discharge is your doctor. Regardless of the managed care plan's policy, the physician treating you must decide when you are medically ready to go home. For example, plans may have targets for how long patients with certain ailments should remain hospitalized. The goal of the targets is to help improve the efficiency of care, ensuring that no one stays in the hospital—which is costly and potentially unhealthy— any longer than necessary. The targets are not, however, hard and fast limits on how long you should stay in the hospital.

Before your admission to the hospital, ask your physician to describe a typical length of stay for a person undergoing treatment similar to yours, as well as what criteria he will use to decide whether you are ready to go home. In fact, throughout the course of your hospitalization, your physician should keep you apprised of your progress and let you know your target discharge date. Your discharge should be driven by your medical condition, not by financial pressure from the managed care plan to send you home to limit expenses. Nor should your physician use financial pressure from the plan— such as a potentially lower annual bonus—as an excuse for sending you home early.

If your physician discharges you prematurely and you suffer complications or are readmitted to the hos-

continued

pital, both your physician and the plan may be liable. The consequences to them may be licensing restrictions or a medical malpractice suit. If you believe you were discharged prematurely, you should lodge a complaint against the plan and your physician with the appropriate state regulatory agency, such as the state attorney general's office, health department or insurance department. (We detail in chapter 7 the individual jurisdictions of these agencies.) You can also contact a qualified malpractice attorney to consider a case against the physician and the plan.

Further, when your admitting physician believes that you are stable enough to return home, you have a right to expect that your physician will discuss a discharge plan with you. He should indicate the self-care steps you will need to take at home, the kind of after-hospital care you will need from him and whether you will need an at-home caregiver to assist your recovery. If you do not have someone to help you after discharge, ask your physician whether he can order home care for a limited period of time following hospitalization.

Most managed care plans offer a home care benefit. Medicare and Medicaid cover home nursing care when it is medically necessary. Even plans that do not have a home care benefit may agree to provide it in exchange for your leaving the hospital as quickly as your safety and health allow. You will, however, need to negotiate this benefit. In the long run, home care visits are less expensive for the plan than continued hospitalization, and most people would rather be home than in a hospital.

MANAGED CARE AND PREGNANCY

Virtually all managed care plans cover prenatal care, labor and delivery, and postpartum care. HMOs are more likely than other types of managed care plans to also offer childbirth classes for expectant parents, as well education on how to care for a new child. These classes can help prepare new parents for their newborn child's health-care needs, including guidance about routine childhood physical exams and immunizations. PPOs, POS plans and managed indemnity plans are less likely to offer these classes. They will, however, usually cover the same prenatal and postpartum medical expenses as HMOs.

Most women in HMOs have lower out-of-pocket expenses for their pregnancy-related care than women in PPOs, POS plans and managed indemnity plans. However, it is critical in the development of the fetus and your health that you not let deductibles or copayments dissuade you from getting all the care you need during a pregnancy. You should take a close look at all the options for prenatal care offered in your managed care plan and opt to use services in the network, which can help reduce your out-of-pocket expenses. If you are in a POS plan, you will be able to choose between the plan's providers and programs (a scenario that results in the lowest cost to you) and out-of-network providers and programs (a scenario that results in the highest costs to you). Unless you have a special need that can best be met by a physician or hospital outside the network, you will save money and probably have better continuity of care by staying in the network.

After—or better yet, before—your child is born, you will choose either a family physician or a pediatrician to manage the many health-care needs growing children have.

MANAGED CARE AND CHILDREN

Managed care can offer some particularly powerful resources for parents and their children. HMOs and PPOs usually cover a full range of health-care services for children, including well-baby care, childhood immunizations and care for acute illnesses.

Managed care models vary in ease of selecting your child's physician. A POS plan allows you to pick a pediatrician or family doctor from its roster of physicians at no additional charge. Or if you wish to incur additional expenses in the form of co-payments and deductibles, you can choose a provider from outside the plan's network. A PPO usually allows you to choose either a family physician or a pediatrician from its list. If you choose a physician not on the PPO's list, you will pay for his services out-of-pocket.

An HMO may offer several choices. It might let you choose a pediatrician as your child's primary care physician. In this case, your child's health-care needs will be managed primarily by that pediatrician, while your needs are managed by a family physician, internist or gynecologist. However, some HMOs might ask that your child's needs be managed by a family physician who seeks assistance from a pediatrician when necessary. In this case, you will likely need a referral from your primary care doctor when your child needs specialized care from a pediatrician.

Once you select a pediatrician or family physician, ask him to outline a care plan for your child that is specifically suited to your child's age and general health. A healthy toddler will have different needs than a teenager with asthma. The doctor's care plan should address both preventive health-care issues, such as immunizations and monitoring physical and intellectual development, as well as the approach to handling common illnesses. You should also ask the physician what health education programs the plan offers that might help you and your child.

If your child has a special or complex problem that requires a pediatric specialist, you should familiarize yourself with the plan's policies for referrals to pediatric specialists. In most PPOs, POS plans and managed indemnity plans, you can usually find a qualified pediatric specialist easily because these plans typically have large networks of physicians from which to choose. In addition, these plans generally let you see someone outside the network, while they still cover at least some of the cost.

Some HMOs, however, have smaller networks of specialty physicians. Thus, there may be fewer pediatric specialists affiliated with the plan. Here is where you need to be careful. Some HMOs may ask you to take your child to a physician who treats only adults—for example, a neurologist instead of a pediatric neurologist. Before you agree, ask the plan and the physician to whom you have been referred to document why he is qualified to handle this pediatric case. If the physician sees children only rarely, rather than regularly, you should refuse to accept this referral. Demand—and formally appeal, if necessary—that the plan locate and cover the costs of a referral to a pediatric specialist in the appropriate field, even if the physician is out of the network.

Beyond any of these basic services, which are part of every managed care plan, there are other health-care services that plans provide. These include a number of special services, such as hospice care, designed to meet specific needs. Chapter 6 takes a look at some of these services typically found in managed care.

6 Using Managed Care to Meet Special Needs

*N*ot all services offered by managed care plans are automatically included in every member's coverage package. While all plan members usually have medical, surgical, hospitalization and preventive services provided, some may have even more. It all depends on whether you or your employer contracts with the plan to purchase the additional services. For example, one employer may want to buy coverage for vision and dental care services, another wants coverage for **alternative health care**, and still another wants to cover hospice care.

Most managed care companies can accommodate any employer's preferences. They do this by having packages specifically crafted to provide these special services. In this chapter, we will look at the special services most often added to basic managed care coverage to help consumers meet their health-care needs.

MANAGED CARE AND MENTAL HEALTH CARE

There is much controversy about whether consumers who need mental health care are treated properly in managed care.

Mental health care benefits in managed care are generally handled by carve-out companies that specialize in mental health services (see chapter 5). These companies develop their own networks of providers. Research shows that a typical provider network is 20 percent psychiatrists, 40 percent psychologists and 40 percent psychiatric social workers. The carve outs also contract with, or operate their own, inpatient mental health facilities. Most consumers in these plans usually are initially treated by the psychologists and social workers, who may then seek assistance from psychiatrists for difficult cases or for consumers who need medications such as antidepressants.

Mental health managed care plans typically have their own hotlines to assist consumers seeking routine services or crisis intervention. They may also have copayments and deductibles that are different from those in your managed care plan.

The company that provides your mental health care coverage will oversee what services you use, and how frequently you use them, to assess whether they are appropriate and necessary. Through utilization review, a mental health managed care plan generally tries to limit the number of days you spend in an inpatient setting to only those necessary to bring your situation under control or to get you started toward rehabilitation. Then your care is moved to an outpatient setting—which is less expensive for the plan—as quickly as possible. The move from inpatient to outpatient care should occur only when inpatient care is clearly no longer needed. If, however, you and your physician believe that a plan is unfairly limiting an inpatient stay, you can appeal the plan's decision. (See chapter 7 for information on the appeal process.) Ultimately, it is up to your physician to decide when you are ready for discharge from an inpatient facility.

The plan also urges your mental health-care providers to treat you according to its protocols for care. The protocols are meant to guide your physician regarding treatment issues such as length of hospital stay, types of medications to use and frequency of counseling visits. We do not yet have enough research to know whether these guidelines improve quality of care or are simply a means of controlling physician behavior in order for the plan to control costs.

Your mental health managed care plan will also ask your physician, psychologist or social worker to document that you are making progress. This is often necessary for the plan to continue to approve services and pay for your care.

MANAGED CARE AND VISION AND DENTAL CARE

Vision and dental services in managed care are also often provided by carve-out companies that specialize in such services. Like the mental health managed care services, these plans assemble their own networks of providers and have their own co-payments and deductibles. They also set limits, often in conjunction with employers, on the services and dollar amounts covered.

Vision Care

Vision managed care plans usually cover three different vision services for consumers: ophthalmologists (physicians who specialize in the diagnosis and treatment of eye diseases), optometrists (clinicians with four years of training at a school of optometry, which allows them to examine the eyes, screen for eye diseases such as glaucoma and prescribe corrective lenses) and opticians (professionals who are trained to make, fit and adjust corrective lenses).

Before we go on to discuss the coverage that most vision managed care plans offer, it is important for you to understand the distinction between optometrists and ophthalmologists. Optometrists are not physicians. They cannot perform surgical procedures such as cataract surgery, and they cannot prescribe medications, although most states allow optometrists during routine eye exams to use drops that make it easier for them to view internal eye structures. Optometrists do not treat eye diseases such as glaucoma and diabetic retinopathy; only ophthalmologists are qualified to diagnose and treat eye diseases and to perform surgical procedures on the eye.

Typically, vision managed care plans cover a complete eye exam every two years and pay for some or all of the costs of corrective lenses for nearsightedness, farsightedness and other focusing problems, which are common in older persons. For this level of care, most plans require consumers to go to optometrists. Some let consumers consult ophthalmologists but require the consumer to pay a higher copayment to see the ophthalmologist. A plan will cover some or all of the cost of corrective lenses if the consumer uses an optician who is in the plan's network.

During a routine eye exam, if your optometrist discovers a medical problem, you will be referred to an ophthalmologist in your plan's network for additional evaluation and treatment. Managed care plans usually cover diagnosis of and treatment for eye diseases and do not subject such care to the limitations of the vision care plans.

Dental Care

Managed care plans that cover dental services are similar to those that cover vision care. They are often carve-out plans that exclusively cover dental care services. The plans have their own networks, or rosters, of dentists, as well as schedules of benefits and covered services. For example, a managed care plan's dental benefits may cover two cleanings and routine exams annually for little or no copayment. Other services, such as fillings, x-rays, extractions and oral surgery, are covered according to a fee schedule. The plan will typically pay part of the fee to the dentist, while the consumer is responsible for the remainder. There may also be an annual deductible, which must be met before coverage begins.

In addition to covering general dental care such as cleanings and checkups, dental managed care plans also cover more complex dental work that many general dentists do not perform. This can include oral surgery (such as having a wisdom tooth extracted), braces for children and treatment of gum disease. If you need any of these kinds of services, your dentist will refer you to a specialist in the dental managed care plan's network—for example, an oral surgeon for an extraction or a periodontist for gum disease. A plan typically has a fee schedule in which the plan pays a portion of an agreed-upon fee to the specialist, while you are responsible for the balance. You may have a lower copayment by seeing a specialist who is a member of the dental managed care plan's network.

MANAGED CARE AND PRESCRIPTION DRUGS

Most consumers in managed care plans have coverage for prescription drugs ordered by physicians. In some cases, the plan itself—such as a health maintenance organization (HMO)—may cover the drug. In other cases, employers who purchase managed care plans for their employees carve out the prescription drug program and contract with a company exclusively in the managed prescription business. These companies are called pharmacy benefit managers (PBMs). If your drug benefit is managed by a PBM, you receive a drug card separate from your managed care plan membership card. It may be used at any pharmacy in the PBM's network of stores or through a mail-order prescription program, which is a common feature of PBMs.

Regardless of whether your prescription drug benefit is administered by your managed care plan or a PBM, be aware of the following:

• The copayment for a prescription drug (usually $5 to $10 per prescription) sometimes varies depending on whether you buy a brand-name drug—a scenario that results in a higher copayment—or a **generic drug**—a scenario that results in a lower copayment. Whenever possible, you should opt for the generic drug to save money. However, first check with your physician and pharmacist to determine if the generic version is appropriate in your case.

While generic drugs are generally as safe and effective as brand-name products, some conditions require you to take the exact same formulation in each dosage. This is something that cannot be controlled in generic drugs.

• If you take a medication regularly, such as a daily pill for blood pressure, your prescription drug plan may offer you the option of buying a one- to three-month supply of the drug by mail order. Such programs generally result in substantial cost savings over retail pharmacies, plus the added convenience of not having to make periodic trips to the drugstore. This is especially helpful if you live in a rural area or have transportation and/or mobility problems.

• A PBM may have a restricted formulary, which means that the plan decides what classes of drugs to cover and creates an exclusive list of products from which consumers and physicians select. This formulary, or list, typically excludes some drugs either because they are more expensive than alternatives or because the plan believes they are ineffective products. These limits sometimes create problems for some consumers, especially if their doctors want them on specific medications not included in the formulary.

If you encounter this situation, you should work with your physician to document for the plan your specific need and why the medication on the formulary is not suitable for you. In most cases, the PBM will approve the drug your doctor orders.

• Prescription drug benefits may have annual dollar limits, which could range from few hundred dollars (typical for Medicare HMOs) to $4,000. While this does not create a burden for most consumers, it is a potential problem for consumers with diseases such as AIDS, where drug therapy can cost $10,000 to $15,000 per year.

If you find that you run up against the dollar limit during the year, there are alternatives. Many pharmaceutical companies offer free drugs to consumers who have no drug coverage or whose benefits for prescription drugs are exhausted. Ask your plan, pharmacist or PBM to help you find a free drug program that can help meet your needs until your pharmacy benefits start again.

• Medicare members who join managed care plans need to be especially watchful about prescription drug benefits. Traditionally, Medicare does not cover oral outpatient drugs, with the exception of certain oral anticancer agents. Thus, one way that Medicare HMOs attract enrollees is to sometimes provide coverage for prescription drugs. The limit on this benefit is usually less generous than the limit for non-Medicare consumers in HMOs—sometimes as little as $500 to $1,000 per year. If in the future the federal government reduces the fees it pays HMOs to enroll Medicare-eligible people, this is one of the services Medicare HMOs might drop since it is an optional benefit.

MANAGED CARE AND ILLNESSES AWAY FROM HOME

In three common situations, you will need to call upon your managed care plan to cover health care when you or a family member is away from home. The first is when you are traveling and are injured or become ill. Clearly, in an emergency, get appropriate medical attention as soon as possible. Then either you or the medical provider who treats you should contact your plan and primary care physician to provide them with a summary of the illness and what was done for you. If you require hospitalization, the provider away from home who treats you, your primary care physician and your plan should work out how and when you can leave the hospital and return home.

If you do require out-of-the-area care while traveling and cannot wait until you get home to see your primary care physician, be prepared to pay physician and hospital bills yourself and then file claims with your managed care plan. Because the providers you see will most likely not be part of your plan's network, they will seek payment directly from you. Any time you receive medical care while traveling, make sure you get the following items from the parties who care for you:

• A detailed bill that includes your diagnosis, all the services provided to you and the charges for the services.

• A copy of any medical records created on your behalf. When you return home to submit a claim to your managed care plan, include a copy of your medical records to demonstrate that the treatment could not have waited until you returned home.

• The names, addresses and phone numbers of all the health-care providers, hospitals and clinics that treated you. You may need this for later contact or claims information.

• The medical license number of the doctor in the state where the care was provided. Insurers, including Medicare, need this to make payment to you.

The second instance in which out-of-the-area medical care is needed is when a dependent child is living away from home—for example, your child is away at school or is living with a divorced parent in one city and is covered by the other parent's managed care plan. A managed care plan usually covers a full-time student living away from home until graduation or until she reaches the age specified in plan enrollment materials. This age is often between 22 and 24 years. To help your student-child use this coverage appropriately, you should read the enrollment materials to see if the following questions are answered:

• What should the student do if she needs medical care and cannot return home to see a local primary care physician?

• How should claims get filed with the plan?

• Will the plan cover the student when she is off from school (such as during summer break or some other time off from school prior to graduation) and then returns to full-time schooling? Will the plan cover a part-time student?

If these and other questions you have are not clearly spelled out in the plan materials, call the plan's customer service number. Ask to have information on the procedures you and your student-child should follow sent to you.

The third circumstance of using managed care to cover illness away from home is when you live part of the year in one location and part in another—a more common occurrence among retirees. If this is your situation and you belong to a point-of-service plan, preferred provider organization or managed indemnity plan, you will encounter few obstacles to receiving care. These types of plans typically pay at least a portion of the costs of care provided by physicians and hospitals that are not part of their networks.

You will, however, have to pay these providers for their services and then file claims with your plan. So ask your plan to supply you with claim forms to use before you switch residences during the year. Further, if you belong to an HMO, ask the plan some questions along the same lines as those outlined earlier for out-of-the-area children.

Make sure you also know whether you can use your pharmacy benefit card out of the area. Call the PBM to find out if it has participating pharmacies in all the areas in which you are a resident. If it does not, you may need to stock up on certain medications before changing residences. Or the PBM may be able to mail your prescription drugs to you upon request and approval of your physician.

MANAGED CARE AND ANCILLARY SERVICES

Consumers often need **ancillary services** to help them recover from illnesses or injuries. Physical, occupational and speech therapy would fall into this realm of care. Most managed care plans cover these services, subject to certain limitations.

A plan typically requires a referral from a physician for you to receive speech, physical or occupational therapy. Your plan may also limit the total number of visits you can make each year to each therapist, as well as require the therapist and your physician to develop a care plan before therapy begins. The plan may wish to see this care plan before your therapy starts in order to preapprove it. Your providers may also have to regularly inform your plan of the progress of your therapy. If you need more visits than your plan allows, you should negotiate this extension with the plan, with help from your therapist and physician. Of course, as with most of the managed care services we have discussed in this chapter, you may have copayments or deductibles that vary from plan to plan.

MANAGED CARE AND THE END OF LIFE

Hospice care is end-of-life supportive care that aids and assists a person with a terminal illness, and assists her family, until the patient's death. Most managed care plans cover hospice care, which can be provided either in the person's home or in an inpatient facility. Check your plan's enrollment materials to see if it covers hospice care. If you cannot find the information you need, contact the plan's customer service office or ask your physician. For the record: Medicare HMOs must cover hospice care.

Hospice care is provided to people for whom aggressive therapy is no longer appropriate or helpful and who are expected to die within six months. The decision about when to stop aggressive medical therapy and start hospice care should be made jointly by the patient, her family and her physician.

If your plan covers hospice, an order from your physician is needed to start hospice care. Hospice care typically includes regular home visits by a registered nurse specifically trained to care for dying patients, medications such as pain relievers to keep the person as comfortable as possible and counseling for the person and her family. If it is not feasible for hospice care to be given at home, some plans admit the person to an inpatient hospice facility they contract with until death comes.

Some managed care plans do not formally cover hospice care. Nonetheless, if you and your physician decide that hospice care is appropriate, you might be able to negotiate it with the plan. You or your physician should contact the plan and ask if, in lieu of paying for additional time in a hospital, the plan would cover home-based or inpatient hospice care. Plans that do not formally cover hospice often will agree to this.

MANAGED CARE AND ALTERNATIVE MEDICINE

There is increasing consumer interest in alternative therapies such as acupuncture, chiropractic, naturopathy and homeopathy. This also is often called complementary medicine. While there is controversy surrounding the medical value of many of these treatments—especially among mainstream medical people— many consumers use and believe in these therapeutic options and often have positive outcomes.

Historically, health insurance plans have been reluctant to cover these services. Managed care plans largely follow this pattern, but many plans are looking more closely at alternative medical care and covering certain services. Check with your plan about what alternative therapies it covers, if any.

The managed care plans that cover certain alternative therapies usually target a specific set of services. For example, a plan may cover a limited number of visits to a chiropractor each year, with a copayment. Some plans now cover a wider range of alternative medical treatments but charge additional premiums to consumers, along with deductibles and copayments. Covered services include nutrition therapy, acupuncture, chiropractic and massage therapy. Because there is increasing consumer demand for these services, you can expect more plans to consider ways to cover alternative medicine.

One bit of advice: It is in your best interest to coordinate your use of alternative therapies with your primary care physician to ensure that all your health care is safe and effective.

7 | Fixing Problems in Managed Care

In the best of all worlds, your experience with and service from your managed care plan will be smooth and trouble free. But like any other business arrangement, things can go wrong.

There will be times when your plan will not live up to your expectations. For example, a dispute may arise when your plan and your physician disagree about a particular test or treatment. The plan may deny payment for something that you and your doctor believe is necessary or refuse to provide you with a service that you believe you are eligible to receive. In these and all other disputes, you should appeal, negotiate or battle with your managed care plan until the matter is resolved.

Consumer complaints about managed care plans are varied. Issues may involve your primary care physician or the way the plan's benefits and policies are implemented. Some of the more common complaints heard include the following:

• The plan or your primary care physician refuses to provide you with a referral to a specialist because he considers such care **medically unnecessary**.

• The plan refuses to pay for a particular test or treatment because the plan considers it ineffective, inappropriate in your case or **experimental**.

• The plan refuses to provide you with access to a specialist who is fully qualified or has enough experience to treat your specific ailment and wants you to see a specialist in the plan's network who is less qualified or inexperienced.

• The plan does not pay its bills to your provider in a timely manner, and a physician or hospital duns you.

• The plan wants you to use a drug from its prescription drug formulary that is different from the product you now use for the same condition and treatment.

• The plan approves your hospitalization for a surgical procedure but then wants you discharged too quickly, in your and/or your doctor's opinion, after the surgery.

When you have a disagreement with your plan, there are several avenues of recourse. In most cases, you should first use the plan's internal grievance or appeals process, which all managed care plans are required to have. If you ask the plan to address a complaint and you are not satisfied with the decision, you can continually appeal the decision up through the hierarchy of the appeals process.

You can also file a complaint against your plan with the appropriate state agency—the insurance department, health department or attorney general's office—or, if necessary, get help from a lawyer. Regardless of the specific situation you face, when you decide to challenge your managed care plan's decision, you must persevere.

USING THE PLAN'S CUSTOMER SERVICE DEPARTMENT

The plan's customer service department is the place to start. All managed care plans have customer service departments to answer questions and resolve minor complaints or misunderstandings with the plans.

Here are some general guidelines when contacting the customer service department.

• Organize your thoughts. Make notes outlining your complaint, including the dates of important events and the names of people involved in the problem, such as your physician, plan employees or a hospital, if one was involved.

• Call the plan's customer service number (it should be listed in your plan's enrollment materials or on the back of your membership card) and explain your concern. You can also let your employer know about your problem by speaking with the person in your workplace who handles your company's health benefits.

• Describe your problem or concern in as much detail as you can. The plan's customer service representative will ask you for a history of the problem, and the better you can document your complaint, the more likely you are to have it addressed quickly and appropriately.

• Ask the representative to tell what specific additional steps you need to take, if any. For many complaints, the customer service representative may be able to help you resolve the question or problem over the phone.

• Ask the plan representative to tell you what steps he will take to address your question and when you can expect to hear from someone in the plan. Make a note of the representative's name, as well as the date and time that you called. Customer service representatives often need to go to other officials in the plan, such as the plan's medical director, to get information or have a decision made on your complaint or question.

• The customer service representative should get back to you within the time period you were told with an answer to your query. If he does not, follow up with the plan and ask to speak with a customer service department supervisor if the delay persists.

• If you are not satisfied with the representative's response to your concerns, ask to speak with a supervisor immediately.

Some complaints and questions cannot be addressed fully over the telephone. In these cases, which usually involve more serious problems such as denial of major surgery or denial of coverage for a new drug, you will need to file a written complaint with the plan. Also, you may wish to file a written complaint if your initial phone inquiry to the plan is unsatisfactory.

WHEN AND HOW TO FILE A WRITTEN COMPLAINT WITH YOUR MANAGED CARE PLAN

When you file your written complaint, depending on its specific nature, a number of different plan officials could review and act on your complaint. If the complaint is not related to quality-of-care concerns but instead deals more with a financial issue such as the plan's nonpayment of a bill, your complaint will most likely be reviewed by the customer service department or by plan officials who oversee the financial and administrative operations.

If your complaint involves a quality-of-care issue such as the plan's denial of medically necessary care, it will move from the customer service department to the plan's medical director. The medical director is a physician who oversees all medical aspects of the plan's operations. The medical director and his staff are responsible for all new policies related to the medical care you receive. The medical director often works in conjunction with committees made up of other plan physicians to review consumers' complaints and to make coverage decisions on specific issues.

The medical director and/or the designated committee reviews your complaint as part of the plan's grievance and appeals procedure—a process that should be outlined in your enrollment materials. (If you cannot locate this information, call the customer service office to get details, including specific directions for how to file a complaint, if you do not already have them.)

An important situation to watch for during an appeal or grievance is whether any of the personnel reviewing your complaint has a conflict of interest. For example, if you are appealing an earlier decision by the medical director over denial of surgery, the medical director should not be part of the appeals process. If anyone does have a conflict, that person's objectivity could be compromised. Ask who is reviewing your complaint. If anyone in that list of people may have previously made an adverse decision that is the basis for your complaint, request that he be excused from the latest review.

PREPARING YOUR GRIEVANCE OR APPEAL

In order to be effective in your grievance or appeal, you must be well prepared. Here are some tips and steps that will help you win your point.

• At the first sign of a problem—for example, your primary care doctor or plan refuses to refer you to a specialist when you believe you need one—start keeping notes. Carefully document each interaction with your physician or other administrators, noting the date of your conversations, what was said and by whom.

• If you disagree with your doctor about a clinical issue, ask him to clearly document in your medical record that you and he disagree. This is critical because your medical record is the official record of what transpires between you and your doctor. While it is his responsibility to maintain the record, it is your right to have your disagreement with him properly documented and also to see what he has written. If he refuses to enter your side of the story into the record, write him a letter documenting your side of the issue and deliver it to his office for placement in your file.

THE ROLE OF SECOND OPINION IN A GRIEVANCE OR APPEAL

If your grievance or appeal is over a clinical judgment made by a primary care physician or specialist, ask the plan to pay for a second opinion from another similarly qualified physician. Getting a second opinion from another primary care physician or specialist may help you resolve your problem without the need to proceed with a grievance or appeal to the plan. Make sure you get authorization for the second opinion in writing from the plan to guard against any later disputes over who should pay for the second opinion.

• Ask your physician for a copy of your medical record, which should include lab results, reports from specialists and other information that may help you document the validity of your complaint. Be aware that not every state has a law guaranteeing consumers access to physician and/or hospital records. You should call your state health department to find out where your state stands on this. If your state has no legislation or other ruling and—for the sake of this example—the provider denies you access to your own record, you may need to consult a lawyer.

Once you assemble your documentation and your notes, you are ready to write your complaint letter (see page 170). Attach copies of pertinent sections of your medical record to your letter, along with any correspondence you may have received from your physician or the plan relating to the matter at hand.

• Mail your letter to the plan official identified in your enrollment materials as the person who handles consumer complaints. Send the letter by certified or registered mail.

• Within seven to 10 days, contact the plan to find out who is handling your complaint and ask how quickly you can expect the plan to act. Because consumers in managed care plans have often complained about how long it takes to get complaints resolved, many plans prioritize complaints. If your complaint involves a quality-of-care issue, ask that the process be speeded up so that there can be a quick resolution. In point of fact, some states require plans to meet specific deadlines when acting on consumer complaints that involve any immediate threat to the life or welfare of an enrollee in the plan. Check with your state insurance or health department for its requirements in this regard.

• Follow up with plan officials frequently to assess the status of your complaint.

• If appropriate to your complaint, ask your primary care physician or specialist to help. Situations in which either or both can help include ones in which the plan refuses to approve a particular test or treatment ordered by the doctor. When this happens, your physician should write his own letter and submit it to plan officials. Make sure you get a copy.

• When your physician submits a letter supporting your grievance or appeal, make sure it is accompanied by copies of any medical studies or other expert opinions (such as letters from specialists) that help document why a disputed test or treatment is appropriate in your case.

• When your plan completes its review, insist that it provide you with a written decision. Do not accept a verbal decision from the plan as resolution of your complaint. If the plan's customer service department or medical director's office calls with a decision, make note of the decision and the caller's name and title and then request a written statement so that there is a permanent record of the plan's action. You should provide a copy of your plan's decision to your physician for placement in your record. This is important if there is confusion later about what the plan

continued on page 173

ANATOMY OF A GOOD COMPLAINT LETTER

Clarity, precision and organization are key to a good complaint letter to a managed care plan or state agency. Look over the following sample complaint letter before you sit down to write your own. Check your enrollment materials or call the plan's customer service phone number to see to whom you should address the letter and where to mail it.

Dear [insert plan official's name]:

I am writing to appeal the denial of payment of a specialist's bill by your plan for services provided to me by XYZ Cardiology Consultants. I also wish to complain about how my primary care physician's office handled my case. My employer is [insert your company's name], and my plan membership number is 111-111-1111. Below is a summary of the events.

• January 28, 1997: I became ill with severe flulike symptoms, including shortness of breath and a severe cough. I treated the cough with over-the-counter medications until February 1, 1997.

• February 1, 1997: I developed chest and shoulder pain in addition to my cough and called my primary care physician, John Jones, M.D. He was not available, and I was told to wait one week for an appointment. Dissatisfied with this answer, I called again several hours later to see if I could get a prescription in lieu of seeing my doctor.

• My physician's partner, Tom Smith, M.D., returned

continued

my call and phoned in a prescription for cough syrup, which I took for five days with no relief.

- February 6, 1997: I finally spoke with my primary care physician, Dr. Jones, who questioned me in detail about my symptoms, which had not abated. He authorized me to proceed immediately to the emergency room at Community General Hospital.

- At the hospital, I was seen by Joe Miller, M.D., of XYZ Cardiology Consultants, who diagnosed me with severe anemia and pericarditis (an inflammation of the sac surrounding the heart). Dr. Miller admitted me to the hospital, where I was treated with intravenous antibiotics for four days. During this hospital stay, I was seen only by Dr. Miller or his partner, Richard Adams, M.D., who communicated with my primary care provider.

- February 10, 1997: Dr. Adams discharged me, with orders for bed rest and a follow-up visit to Dr. Miller in two days. I was seen February 12, 1997, by Dr. Miller and authorized to return to work on February 13, 1997. He said he did not need to see me again.

To date, your plan has refused to cover the cost of the follow-up visit to Dr. Miller, after my release from the hospital. I have had three conversations with your customer service office since I started getting bills from the cardiologists' billing agency a month after my release from the hospital. These phone calls took place on March 15, 20 and 27, 1997.

I received contradictory information in the calls. Twice I was told that the bill would be paid by your plan. In the third call, I was told that the posthospitalization visit to Dr. Miller was an unauthorized visit to a special-

continued

ist, for which I am responsible. The bill is for $135 and is now being pursued by a collection agency, which is threatening action in small claims court to collect the bill.

I am also disappointed by the way my primary care physician's office handled my complaint of chest pain, shortness of breath and severe cough. I believe that I should have been given a priority appointment to see Dr. Jones, which could have prevented my hospitalization in the first place.

Attached are copies of the bill, the discharge note from my hospitalization, a letter from Dr. Miller to Dr. Jones summarizing my hospital stay and outlining a care plan, and my notes from my conversations with your customer service department. I followed plan rules, and at no time did Dr. Jones, my primary care physician, inform me that I would need an additional referral authorization from him for a single posthospitalization visit to Dr. Miller. In light of this series of events and the fact that Dr. Miller did not release me from his care until my follow-up visit with him, I believe the plan should pay the cost of the visit. I look forward to hearing the results of your review of this matter within 10 business days.

Sincerely,

Managed care plan consumer

cc: State attorney general
     State insurance department
     State health department
     State medical licensing board

Source: Health Education and Advocacy Unit of the Maryland
         Attorney General's Office.

told you, if the plan reneges on its decision or if you later pursue legal action against the plan.

• If you are not satisfied with your plan's decision, discuss the matter with your physician and consider pursuing the complaint with the state government agency that oversees complaints against managed care plans. If you are in a Medicare or Medicaid health maintenance organization (HMO), you may have special appeal rights available to you. Here are some consumer-savvy tips for following through.

Complaint-Resolution Tips for Medicare HMO Enrollees

With more Medicare beneficiaries enrolling in Medicare health maintenance organizations (HMOs), it has been reported that many people are having problems getting their complaints addressed quickly and thoroughly. In October 1996, a federal judge in Arizona ruled that the federal government's rules for complaint resolution by Medicare HMOs are not adequate to protect enrollees. As a result of the order, however, the federal government drafted new rules for Medicare HMOs.

The new rules were proposed on April 30, 1997, and give enrollees access to quick appeals when they believe their HMOs have unfairly denied coverage or otherwise denied them benefits they were entitled to. If you are a Medicare enrollee, these are some expected features you should know about.

• Medicare HMOs must have procedures that give enrollees an expedited appeals process of no more than 72 hours in any situation that "could affect the life or health of the enrollee or the enrollee's ability to regain maximum function." Thus, a health plan could take only 24 or 48 hours to handle an appeal of a denial of service, but must take no more than 72 hours and must provide the enrollee with written decision.

• Medicare HMOs can have an extension of up to 10 days beyond the 72-hour requirement, if the extension is beneficial to the Medicare HMO member. For instance, if the additional time lets the enrollee get additional diagnostic tests, consult specialists or gather additional information, the plan can extend its decision-making period.

• A Medicare HMO enrollee who seeks an expedited appeal of a plan decision should always do so through a physician who is affiliated with the Medicare HMO he belongs to. If the request for a review by the plan comes from a physician who is not affiliated with the plan, there may be a delay. In this situation, the 72-hour countdown does not start until *after* the plan receives all the necessary medical information from the physician. Thus, if the physician does not send the information, or if the plan says it never received it, the plan does not have to meet the 72-hour standard.

• When it comes to discharge from the hospital, Medicare HMO enrollees have two forms of protection. While you can use the appeal process outlined above, you can also still request an immediate review of a plan decision that may lead to an inappropriately short hospital stay. The review is conducted by a peer review organization, or PRO. If you are hospitalized and believe you are being discharged too soon, seek a review by the PRO first, before asking the plan to undertake any other internal review. Hospital and plan officials should both have the information necessary for you to initiate an appeal through the PRO.

These new Medicare rules for how Medicare HMOs must handle enrollees' complaints took effect in August 1997, after a period of public comment. If you are a Medicare enrollee, and you need help now with a problem with your HMO, you can turn to several resources.

• Your local health insurance counseling program (see Appendix D for a list of phone numbers). Each state has one of these programs, funded by the federal government, to help Medicare enrollees with problems related to their traditional

Medicare coverage or Medicare HMOs. This office can help you write a complaint against a Medicare HMO.

• Your local Social Security office or regional HCFA office. Check your phone book for their phone numbers.

• The Medicare hotline (800-638-6833)

• Your state regulatory agencies—insurance department, health department and attorney general's office—or your congressional representative

A final point on the proposed Medicare rules: In March 1997, the inspector general of the U.S. Department of Health and Human Services reported that more than half of Medicare HMOs do not comply even with current federal rules on handling grievances and appeals. She reported that many Medicare enrollees were never even informed that they had a right to appeal adverse decisions by their Medicare HMOs. So remember: *All Medicare HMO enrollees have a right to appeal their Medicare HMOs' decisions.*

Complaint-Resolution Tips for Medicaid HMO Enrollees

Fewer complaint-resolution resources are available to Medicaid HMO enrollees than to Medicare HMO enrollees. This is because the individual states decide what types of grievance and appeals procedures each wants to have.

If you want to file a complaint against a Medicaid HMO, contact the plan and your state Medicaid office to learn what rules and procedures to follow. In some states, local (county or city) health departments are setting up ombudsman programs to help Medicaid enrollees deal with managed care problems. The ombudsman is an official troubleshooter whose job is to help a Medicaid enrollee file a complaint and then to work with the plan to resolve the issue. Maryland, for example, is planning to have a program in which there is one ombudsman in every county to help Medicaid HMO enrollees in that county. Other states are considering similar approaches. Check with your state Medicaid office to see what is available to you.

If your state does not have an ombudsman program, you can still use all the other state resources available to you to help resolve a problem with your Medicaid HMO: the state attorney general's office, insurance and health departments and Medicaid office.

GETTING HELP FROM STATE GOVERNMENT AGENCIES

Every state has one or more agencies that regulate managed care plans and help consumers resolve complaints against the plans. Unfortunately, because each state writes its own laws and regulations, there are wide variations from state to state in what agencies can help you. Throughout this book, we have mentioned three state agencies that have the greatest oversight of managed care plans: the attorney general's office, the insurance department and the health department. How much authority each office has over managed care plans in your state depends on your state's laws. In most states, however, insurance departments license managed care plans, monitor their financial health and review their contracts and marketing materials. Health departments typically oversee the quality of care that managed care plans provide. The health department also assesses the quality of care provided by the doctors and hospitals affiliated with the plans. Finally, in most states, the attorney general is the chief law enforcement officer, who can investigate and prosecute potential violations of state law. Many attorney generals also have consumer-protection divisions that can help consumers who have complaints against managed care plans.

You can approach a state agency with your complaint about a plan in any of three ways.

- You can call the agency and register a complaint or ask your question over the phone. Some agencies answer basic questions over the phone but will require a written statement if you want to pursue the issue.

- You can send the agency copies of the complaint letter you sent to your managed care plan. (Be sure to also send the plan a copy of your letter to the regulatory agency.) This allows the agency to file your complaint and also starts the review process by agency officials. If you provide such data, the agency may decide to intervene or act on your behalf right away. Or it may wait to see if your plan resolves the problem satisfactorily.

- The third way to apprise a state agency of your complaint is to wait until your managed care plan makes its decision on your complaint. Then if you and the plan still disagree, you should file a complaint with one of the government agencies noted above. You will need to include your original letter of complaint to the plan, as well as all supporting documents (such as your notes and letters from physicians) and a copy of the plan's decision in response to your original complaint letter. Organize this information into an easy-to-read packet for your state agency and send it to the agency. Make sure you send only photocopies of the documents and keep all the originals.

Each state agency has its own protocol for reviewing complaints against managed care plans. However, each will review the complaint to determine how serious it is and decide what internal resources to devote to it.

Some states have taken an aggressive approach to complaint resolution by giving consumers in managed care plans specific grievance and appeal rights. New York and New Jersey, for example, have passed legislation creating specific requirements that managed care plans must meet regarding how they review and act on consumers' complaints. The New York law establishes minimum standards for plans' complaint procedures and also specifies how quickly plans must act on complaints. In cases where a consumer's health is at risk, the plan must act within 48 hours. New Jersey has gone one step further by setting up an independent appeals panel that consumers use for problems with their HMOs. Other states, including Connecticut and Maryland, are overhauling their complaint investigation processes to meet the demands of the growing numbers of consumers in managed care plans.

GETTING HELP FOR COMPLAINTS AGAINST SELF-INSURED MANAGED CARE PLANS

In some complaints, however, state agencies can do little to help you. As we explained in chapter 3, some managed care plans are self-insured plans. These plans are owned by employers who are exempt from state laws governing many aspects of health insurance. If you have a complaint against a self-insured plan, you can expect little or no help from federal or state government agencies after first trying to resolve the complaint with the plan.

Self-insured managed care plans (ask your employer or the plan if your managed care plan is self-insured—the larger your employer, the more likely your plan is self-insured) are not subject to regulation by any of the three state agencies we've discussed (health department, insurance department or attorney general's office). This is because of ERISA (the Employee Retirement Income Security Act), which stipulates that only federal agencies such as the U.S. Department of Labor (DOL) can help consumers resolve complaints against self-insured managed care plans. Unfortunately, in many instances, the DOL provides very little assistance.

If your plan is self-insured, you should still start with the plan's internal complaint-resolution process. Most complaints do get resolved this way. If, however, the plan's decision is unsatisfactory and you wish to pursue it further, you may need to raise the issue directly with your employer. Ask your company to intervene on your behalf with the managed care plan. This is often effective because your employer is actually paying all the healthcare bills incurred by plan members and plays a key role in developing plan procedures and rules.

The DOL may offer some assistance depending on the specifics of your problem. You can reach the department at 202-219-8776 to ask if it can help with your specific situation and to find out how and where to file a complaint against a self-insured managed care plan. Whether or not the DOL can help you depends on your complaint. For example, if your complaint is that your employer has been collecting health insurance premiums from your paycheck but is not providing health benefits, the DOL can refer the complaint to a field enforcement office for review.

If, however, your complaint is that the plan has denied a service you believe is a covered benefit and medically necessary or that the plan has not paid a claim in a timely manner, the DOL will not likely be able to help you, beyond making an exploratory phone call or two on your behalf. Most consumers who call with this type of complaint are advised by the DOL to try to resolve the issue with their employers and plan or to pursue the complaint in federal court. The DOL does not provide consumers with individual complaint investigation or resolution for these types of complaints.

In the event that you need to pursue a complaint against a self-insured plan in federal court, you must find an attorney who is experienced in ERISA issues. Check with your local bar association to locate a lawyer who can help you.

All is not as grim as it might seem, however. There are signs that consumers in self-insured plans will soon have more help available to them. The federal government has started a demonstration project in Oklahoma that allows the state insurance department to help consumers who have complaints against self-insured health plans. This special agreement, in which the department works with the DOL and managed care plans to review complaints, may provide an avenue of relief for consumers in self-insured managed care plans that was previously unavailable to them. Other states are interested in participating in this project to provide assistance to consumers in self-insured plans in their jurisdictions, so the project may expand to other states in the future.

EPILOGUE

Using Managed Care Wisely
and Making the System Work

*M*anaged care as a way of delivering and paying for health care is here to stay, but it is also a work in progress. Managed care plans will continue to evolve, and we will no doubt see more, and more innovative, managed care plans in the future. Each will offer you unique advantages and disadvantages, and it is up to you to learn the details of each plan to decide how well it will meet your needs and at what cost.

Regardless of changes in managed care plans or your personal views on managed care, one thing should remain constant: Your satisfaction in managed care requires that you take an active role. From evaluating and selecting a plan and health-care providers, to using plan offerings wisely, to challenging plan decisions that you believe are incorrect, managed care has ushered in a new era of challenge and responsibility for health-care consumers.

When you choose a managed care plan, you are making a decision that is both complex and important. By enrolling in a managed care plan, you are committing your money and trust to a company that you may one day need to protect your health and welfare. This is not a trivial decision. Health plans are more complex today than in the past, and the sheer size and power of the managed care industry will have a major influence on the health care you receive.

It will take consumers time to adjust to managed care. Likewise, it will take plans time to reshape the health-care market. Some changes brought about by managed care will no doubt benefit consumers by restraining costs and improving quality. In other cases, the industry will learn important lessons about the limits of what consumers will tolerate. It will learn those lessons, however, only if you and others are willing to voice your concerns and expectations. Through this dialogue, which will occur in workplaces, union halls, managed care plans' administrative offices and physicians' offices and before legislators, consumers' demands for appropriate, compassionate, high-quality care will prompt the industry to identify more creative ways to deliver it and create and preserve a consumer-centered health-care system.

Getting high-quality, affordable health care is not something you can solely entrust to others—not to plan administrators, physicians or even employers. When you take an assertive, active role in your managed care plan, you increase the likelihood that your managed care plan will meet your needs. Remember these five points about coping and being satisfied with managed care.

1. Carefully list and put in priority your health-care needs before you enroll in a managed care plan or choose health-care providers.

2. Take the time to evaluate your managed care plan options, using our guidelines in chapter 3, and measure them against your specific needs.

3. Choose your health-care providers carefully along the criteria we identify in chapter 4 and work to build an honest, open relationship with them.

4. Make sure you give feedback on your satisfaction with your plan and your providers to the plan and to your employer's benefits manager. It is important for you to take the time to answer consumer satisfaction surveys that many plans and some employers and state government agencies sponsor.

5. Take action when problems arise with your plan or your health-care providers. The managed care market is extremely competitive, and most plans and providers will work hard to resolve disputes and satisfy your needs to ensure that they do not lose your, or your employer's, business. When all else fails, contact government agencies or an attorney to help resolve your problem.

Finally, remember that this period of great change in health care also presents you with great opportunity. Never before have consumers had so many chances to learn so much about health care and make choices that can help the market work better. By defending your interests and exercising your power as a consumer through well-informed choices, you will help shape this market and make it more responsive to your needs.

APPENDIX A

State Attorney Generals' Offices

ALABAMA

Attorney General
11 S. Union St.
Montgomery, AL 36130
334-242-7300

ALASKA

Attorney General
Office of the Attorney General
P.O. Box 110300
Juneau, AK 99811
907-465-3600

ARIZONA

Attorney General
Office of the Attorney General
1275 W. Washington St.
Phoenix, AZ 85007
602-542-4266

ARKANSAS

Attorney General
Office of the Attorney General
Little Rock, AR 72201
501-682-2007

CALIFORNIA

Attorney General
Office of the Attorney General
1200 I St.
Sacramento, CA 95814
916-324-5437

COLORADO

Attorney General
Office of the Attorney General
1625 Broadway, Suite 1700
Denver, CO 80202
303-620-4500

CONNECTICUT

Attorney General
Office of the Attorney General
55 Elm St.
Hartford, CT 06106
860-566-2026

DELAWARE

Attorney General
Office of the Attorney General
Carvel State Office Building
820 N. French St.
Wilmington, DE 19801
302-577-3838

DISTRICT OF COLUMBIA

Attorney General
Office of the Corporation
   Counsel
441 Fourth St., N.W.
Washington, DC 20001
202-727-6248

FLORIDA

Attorney General
Office of the Attorney General
The Capitol, PL01
Tallahassee, FL 32399-1050
904-487-1963

GEORGIA

Attorney General
Office of the Attorney General
40 Capitol Square, S.W.
Atlanta, GA 30334-1300
404-656-4584

HAWAII

Attorney General
Office of the Attorney General
425 Queen St.
Honolulu, HI 96813
808-586-1282

IDAHO

Attorney General
Office of the Attorney General
P.O. Box 83720
Boise, ID 83720-0010
208-334-2400

ILLINOIS

Attorney General
Office of the Attorney General
500 S. Second St.
Springfield, IL 62706
217-782-1090

INDIANA

Attorney General
Office of the Attorney General
402 W. Washington St.
Indianapolis, IN 46205
317-232-6201

IOWA

Attorney General
Office of the Attorney General
Hoover Office Building,
   Second Floor
Des Moines, IA 50319
515-281-8373

KANSAS
Attorney General
Office of the Attorney General
301 W. 10th Ave.
Judicial Center
Topeka, KS 66612
913-296-2215

KENTUCKY
Attorney General
Office of the Attorney General
700 Capitol Building
Frankfort, KY 40601
502-564-7600

LOUISIANA
Attorney General
Office of the Attorney General
P.O. Box 94005
Baton Rouge, LA 70804
504-342-7013

MAINE
Attorney General
Office of the Attorney General
State House Station 6
Augusta, ME 04333
207-626-8800

MARYLAND
Attorney General
Office of the Attorney General
200 St. Paul Place
Baltimore, MD 21202
410-576-6300

MASSACHUSETTS
Attorney General
Office of the Attorney General
One Ashburton Place
Boston, MA 02108
617-727-2200

MICHIGAN
Attorney General
Office of the Attorney General
P.O. Box 30212
Lansing, MI 48909
517-373-1110

MINNESOTA
Attorney General
Office of the Attorney General
102 State Capitol
St. Paul, MN 55155
612-296-6198

MISSISSIPPI
Attorney General
Office of the Attorney General
P.O. Box 220
Jackson, MS 32905
601-359-3680

MISSOURI
Attorney General
Office of the Attorney General
Supreme Court Building
P.O. Box 899
Jefferson City, MO 65102
314-751-3321

MONTANA

Attorney General
Office of the Attorney General
Department of Justice
P.O. Box 201401
Helena, MT 59620
406-444-2026

NEBRASKA

Attorney General
Office of the Attorney General
P.O. Box 98920
2115 State Capitol Building
Lincoln, NE 68509-8920
402-471-2682

NEVADA

Attorney General
Office of the Attorney General
Capitol Complex
198 S. Capitol St.
Carson City, NV 89710
702-687-3510

NEW HAMPSHIRE

Attorney General
Office of the Attorney General
33 Capitol St.
Concord, NH 03301
603-271-3655

NEW JERSEY

Attorney General
Office of the Attorney General
Hughes Justice Complex,
   CN 080
Trenton, NJ 08625
609-292-4925

NEW MEXICO

Attorney General
Office of the Attorney General
P.O. Drawer 1508
Santa Fe, NM 87504-1508
505-827-6000

NEW YORK

Attorney General
Office of the Attorney General
State Capitol
Albany, NY 12224
518-474-7330

NORTH CAROLINA

Attorney General
Office of the Attorney General
P.O. Box 629
Raleigh, NC 27601
919-733-3377

NORTH DAKOTA

Attorney General
Office of the Attorney General
State Capitol, First Floor
600 East Boulevard
Bismarck, ND 58505-0040
701-328-2210

OHIO
Attorney General
Office of the Attorney General
30 E. Broad St., 17th Floor
Columbus, OH 43215
614-466-3376

OKLAHOMA
Attorney General
Office of the Attorney General
2300 N. Lincoln Blvd., Suite 112
Oklahoma City, OK 73105
405-521-3921

OREGON
Attorney General
Office of the Attorney General
1162 Court St., N.E.
Salem, OR 97310
503-378-6002

PENNSYLVANIA
Attorney General
Office of the Attorney General
Strawberry Square, 16th Floor
Fourth and Walnut Streets
Harrisburg, PA 17120
717-787-3391

PUERTO RICO
Attorney General
P.O. Box 192
San Juan, PR 00902
809-721-7700

RHODE ISLAND
Attorney General
Office of the Attorney General
72 Pine St.
Providence, RI 02903
401-274-4400

SOUTH CAROLINA
Attorney General
P.O. Box 11549
Columbia, SC 29211
803-734-3970

SOUTH DAKOTA
Attorney General
State Capitol
500 E. Capitol Ave.
Pierre, SD 57501
605-773-3215

TENNESSEE
Attorney General
450 James Robertson Pkwy.
Nashville, TN 37243-0485
615-741-3491

TEXAS
Attorney General
300 W. 15th St.
Austin, TX 78701
512-463-2100

UTAH

Attorney General
236 State Capitol
Salt Lake City, UT 84114
801-538-1015

VERMONT

Attorney General
Pavilion Office Building
109 State St.
Montpelier, VT 05602
802-828-3171

VIRGINIA

Attorney General
Office of the Attorney General
900 E. Main
Richmond, VA 23219
804-786-2071

VIRGIN ISLANDS

Attorney General
Office of the Attorney General
Gers Complex, Second Floor
46 Norre Gade
St. Thomas, VI 00802
809-774-5666

WASHINGTON

Attorney General
Office of the Attorney General
Highway-Licenses Building
Seventh Floor, MS PB-71
Olympia, WA 98504
360-493-2006

WEST VIRGINIA

Attorney General
Office of the Attorney General
State Capitol
Building 1, Room 26 East
Charleston, WV 25305-0220
304-558-2021

WISCONSIN

Attorney General
Office of the Attorney General
114 E. State Capitol
P.O. Box 7857
Madison, WI 53707-7857
608-266-1221

WYOMING

Attorney General
Office of the Attorney General
123 State Capitol
Cheyenne, WY 82002
307-777-7841

APPENDIX B

State Health Departments

ALABAMA

Health Department
Public Health Department
434 Monroe St.
Montgomery, AL 36130-1701
334-613-5300

ALASKA

Department of Health
Health and Social Services
  Department
P.O. Box 110601
Juneau, AK 99811
907-465-3030

ARIZONA

Health Department
Department of Health Services
1740 W. Adams St.
Phoenix, AZ 85007
602-542-1000

ARKANSAS

Department of Health
Health Department
4815 W. Markham St., Slot 41
Little Rock, AR 72205-3867
501-661-2112

CALIFORNIA

Department of Health
Health and Welfare Agency
714 P St., Room 1253
Sacramento, CA 95234-7320
916-445-4171

COLORADO

Department of Health
Health Care Policy and
  Financing Department
1575 Sherman St.
Denver, CO 80203-1714
303-866-2993

CONNECTICUT

Department of Health
Public Health Department
150 Washington St.
Hartford, CT 06106
860-566-2038

DELAWARE

Department of Health
Health and Social Services
    Department
2055 Limestone Rd., Suite 300
Wilmington, DE 19808
302-995-8630

DISTRICT OF COLUMBIA

Department of Health
Department of Human Services
1660 L St., N.W., Suite 1200
Washington, DC 20036
202-673-7700

FLORIDA

Department of Health
Health and Rehabilitative
    Services Department
1317 Winewood Blvd.
Tallahassee, FL 32399-0700
904-487-2705

GEORGIA

Department of Health
Human Resources Department
2 Peachtree St., N.W.
Atlanta, GA 30303
404-657-2700

HAWAII

Department of Health
Health Department
1250 Punchbowl St.
Honolulu, HI 96813-3378
808-586-4410

IDAHO

Department of Health
Health and Welfare Department
Towers Building, Fourth Floor
Boise, ID 83720
208-334-5945

ILLINOIS

Department of Health
Public Health Department
535 W. Jefferson St.
Springfield, IL 62761
217-782-4977

INDIANA

Department of Health
Health Department
1330 W. Michigan St.
Indianapolis, IN 42606-1964
317-383-6100

IOWA

Department of Health
Public Health Department
Lucas State Office Building
Des Moines, IA 50319
515-281-5605

KANSAS
Department of Health
Health and Environment
  Department
Landon State Office Building
Topeka, KS 66612
913-296-1500

KENTUCKY
Health Department
Human Resources Cabinet
275 E. Main St.
Frankfort, KY 40621
502-564-3970

LOUISIANA
Health Department
Health and Hospitals
  Department
325 Loyola Ave.
New Orleans, LA 70160
504-568-5050

MAINE
Department of Health
Human Services Department
State House Station 11
Augusta, ME 04333-0011
207-287-3201

MARYLAND
Department of Health
Health and Mental Hygiene
  Department
201 W. Preston St.
Baltimore, MD 21201
410-225-6500

MASSACHUSETTTS
Department of Health
Health and Human Services
  Executive Office
250 Washington St.
Boston, MA 02108-4619
617-624-5200

MICHIGAN
Department of Health
Public Health Department
3423 Martin Luther King Blvd.
Lansing, MI 48909
517-335-8000

MINNESOTA
Department of Health
Public Health Department
P.O. Box 9441
Minneapolis, MN 55440
612-623-5000

MISSISSIPPI
Department of Health
Health Department
P.O. Box 1700
Jackson, MS 39215-1700
601-960-7400

MISSOURI
Department of Health
P.O. Box 570
Jefferson City, MO 65102
314-751-6001

MONTANA
Department of Health
Department of Health and
   Environment
P.O. Box 200901
Helena, MT 59620-0901
406-444-2544

NEBRASKA
Department of Health
P.O. Box 95007
Lincoln, NE 68509
402-471-2133

NEVADA
Department of Health
Human Resources Department
Director's Office, Room 600
Carson City, NV 89710
702-687-4400

NEW HAMPSHIRE
Department of Health
Health and Human Services
   Department
Health and Welfare Building
Concord, NH 03301-6527
603-271-4501

NEW JERSEY
Department of Health
Health and Agriculture Building
Trenton, NJ 08625
609-292-7837

NEW MEXICO
Department of Health
Health Department
P.O. Box 261
Santa Fe, NM 87505
505-827-2389

NEW YORK
Department of Health
Corning Tower, Room 1408
Albany, NY 12237
518-474-2011

NORTH CAROLINA
Department of Health
Environment, Health and Natural
   Resources Department
P.O. Box 27687
Raleigh, NC 27611
919-733-4984

NORTH DAKOTA
Department of Health
Department of Health and
   Consolidated Laboratories
State Capitol, Judicial Wing
Bismarck, ND 58505-0200
701-224-2372

OHIO
Department of Health
Health Department
246 N. High St.
Columbus, OH 43215
614-466-3543

OKLAHOMA
Department of Health
Health Department
1000 N.E. 10th St.
Oklahoma City, OK 73117
405-271-4200

OREGON
Department of Health
Department of Human
  Resources
800 N.E. Oregon St.
Portland, OR 97214
503-731-4000

PENNSYLVANIA
Department of Health
Health Department
Health and Welfare Building
Harrisburg, PA 17108
717-787-6436

PUERTO RICO
Department of Health
P.O. Box 70184
San Juan, PR 00928
809-766-1892

RHODE ISLAND
Department of Health
Health Department
3 Capitol Hill
Providence, RI 02908-5097
401-277-2231

SOUTH CAROLINA
Department of Health
2600 Bull St.
Columbia, SC 29201
803-734-4880

SOUTH DAKOTA
Department of Health
445 E. Capitol Ave.
Pierre, SD 57501-3185
605-773-3361

TENNESSEE
Department of Health
Tennessee Tower, Ninth Floor
Nashville, TN 37247-0101
615-741-3111

TEXAS
Department of Health
1100 W. 49th St.
Austin, TX 78756
512-458-7375

UTAH
Department of Health
288 N. 1460 West
Salt Lake City, UT 84116-0700
801-538-6101

VERMONT
Department of Health
Human Services Agency
P.O. Box 70
Burlington, VT 05402
802-863-7280

VIRGINIA
Department of Health
P.O. Box 2440
Main Street Station
Richmond, VA 23218
804-786-3561

VIRGIN ISLANDS
Department of Health
Health Department
48 Sugar Estates
St. Thomas, VI 00802
809-776-8311

WASHINGTON
Department of Health
Health Department
P.O. Box 47890
Olympia, WA 98504-7890
360-753-5871

WEST VIRGINIA
Department of Health
Health and Human Resources
    Department
State Capitol Complex
Charleston, WV 25305
304-558-0684

WISCONSIN
Department of Health
Health and Social Services
    Department
P.O. Box 7850
Madison, WI 53707
608-266-9622

WYOMING
Department of Health
Health Department
Hathaway Building
Cheyenne, WY 82002
307-777-7656

APPENDIX C

State Insurance Departments

ALABAMA

Insurance Department
Retirement Systems Building
135 S. Union St.
Montgomery, AL 36130-4301
334-269-3550

ALASKA

Insurance Department
Division of Insurance
P.O. Box 11805
333 Willoughby Ave.,
 Ninth Floor
Juneau, AK 99811-0805
907-465-2515

ARIZONA

Insurance Department
Office of the Commissioner
2910 N. 44th St., Suite 210
Phoenix, AZ 85018
602-912-8400

ARKANSAS

Insurance Department
Office of the Commissioner
University Tower Building,
 Room 400
1123 S. University Ave.
Little Rock, AR 72204
501-686-2945

CALIFORNIA

Insurance Department
Department of Insurance
300 S. Spring St.
Los Angeles, CA 90013
213-897-8921

COLORADO

Insurance Department
Division of Insurance
1560 Broadway, Suite 850
Denver, CO 80202
303-894-7499

CONNECTICUT

Insurance Department
Office of the Commissioner
P.O. Box 816
Hartford, CT 06142-0816
860-297-3800

DELAWARE

Insurance Department
Office of the Commissioner
841 Silver Lake Blvd.
Dover, DE 19903
302-739-4251

DISTRICT OF COLUMBIA

Insurance Department
Consumer and Regulatory
    Affairs Department
613 G St., N.W., Sixth Floor
Washington, DC 20001
202-727-8000

FLORIDA

Insurance Department
Office of the Commissioner
The Capitol
Tallahassee, FL 32399-0300
904-922-3100

GEORGIA

Insurance Department
Office of the Commissioner
2 Martin Luther King Jr. Dr.
West Tower, Seventh Floor
Atlanta, GA 30334
404-656-2056

HAWAII

Insurance Department
Commerce and Consumer
    Affairs Department
P.O. Box 3614
Honolulu, HI 96813
808-586-2790

IDAHO

Insurance Department
Office of the Director
P.O. Box 83720
Boise, ID 83720-0043
208-334-4250

ILLINOIS

Insurance Department
Office of the Director
320 W. Washington St.
Springfield, IL 62767
217-782-4515

INDIANA

Insurance Department
Office of the Commissioner
311 W. Washington St., Suite 300
Indianapolis, IN 46204-2787
317-232-2385

IOWA

Insurance Department
Commerce Department
Lucas State Office Building,
    Sixth Floor
Des Moines, IA 50319
515-281-5705

KANSAS
Insurance Department
Office of the Commissioner
420 S.W. Ninth St.
Topeka, KS 66612
913-296-3071

KENTUCKY
Insurance Department
Office of the Commissioner
229 W. Main St.
P.O. Box 517
Frankfort, KY 40602
502-564-3630

LOUISIANA
Insurance Department
Office of the Commissioner
P.O. Box 94214
Baton Rouge, LA 70804-9214
504-342-5900
800-259-5300

MAINE
Insurance Department
Professional and Financial
 Regulation Department
State House Station 35
Augusta, ME 04333
207-624-8475

MARYLAND
Insurance Department
Insurance Division
501 St. Paul Place
Baltimore, MD 21202
410-333-6225

MASSACHUSETTS
Insurance Department
Consumer Affairs and Business
 Regulation Executive Office
470 Atlantic Ave.
Boston, MA 02110
617-521-7777

MICHIGAN
Insurance Department
Insurance Bureau
Ottawa Building, Second Floor
P.O. Box 30220
Lansing, MI 48909-7720
517-373-9273

MINNESOTA
Insurance Department
Insurance Division
133 E. Seventh St.
St. Paul, MN 55101
612-296-4026

MISSISSIPPI
Insurance Department
1804 Walter Sillers Building
550 High St.
Jackson, MS 39205
601-359-3569

MISSOURI
Insurance Department
Division of Insurance
Truman State Office Building
301 W. High St., Suite 630
Jefferson City, MO 65101
314-751-2640

MONTANA

Insurance Department
Commissioner of Insurance
P.O. Box 4009
Helena, MT 59604
406-444-2040

NEBRASKA

Insurance Department
Department of Insurances
941 O St., Suite 400
Lincoln, NE 68508
402-471-2201

NEVADA

Insurance Department
Department of Business
  and Industry
1665 Hot Springs Rd.,
  Room 152
Carson City, NV 98710
702-687-4270

NEW HAMPSHIRE

Insurance Department
169 Manchester St.
Concord, NH 03301
603-271-2261

NEW JERSEY

Insurance Department
Division of Administration
Mary Roebling Building,
  12th Floor
20 W. State St.
Trenton, NJ 08625
609-292-5360

NEW MEXICO

Insurance Department
Department of Insurance
Pera Building
P.O. Drawer 1269
Santa Fe, NM 87504-1269
505-827-4500

NEW YORK

Insurance Department
Office of the Commissioner
160 W. Broadway
New York, NY 10013
212-602-0429

NORTH CAROLINA

Insurance Department
Department of Insurance
P.O. Box 26387
430 N. Salisbury St.
Raleigh, NC 27611
919-733-7343

NORTH DAKOTA

Insurance Department
State Capitol, Fifth Floor
600 East Blvd.
Bismarck, ND 58505-0320
701-328-2440

OHIO

Insurance Department
Department of Insurance
2100 Stella Court
Columbus, OH 43215-1067
614-644-2658

OKLAHOMA

Insurance Department
State Insurance Building
1901 N. Walnut Blvd.
Oklahoma City, OK 73152
405-521-2828

OREGON

Insurance Department
Insurance and Finance Division
440-2 Labor and Industry
  Building
Salem, OR 97310
503-378-4474
503-378-4636

PENNSYLVANIA

Insurance Department
Department of Insurance
1321 Strawberry Square
Fourth and Walnut Streets
Harrisburg, PA 17120
717-787-2317

PUERTO RICO

Insurance Department
Office of the Commissioner
1607 Ponce de Leon Ave.,
  Stop 23
P.O. Box 8330
Santurce, PR 00959
809-722-8686

RHODE ISLAND

Insurance Department
Office of the Commissioner
233 Richmond St., Suite 233
Providence, RI 02903-4237
401-277-2223
401-277-2246

SOUTH CAROLINA

Insurance Department
Office of the Commissioner
1612 Marion St.
P.O. Box 100105
Columbia, SC 29202-3105
803-737-6160
803-737-6268

SOUTH DAKOTA

Insurance Department
Department of Commerce
  and Regulation
Insurance Division
500 E. Capitol Ave.
Pierre, SD 57501
605-773-4104

TENNESSEE

Insurance Department
500 James Robertson Pkwy.
Nashville, TN 37243-0600
615-741-4737
800-342-8385

TEXAS

Insurance Department
Texas Department of Insurance
P.O. Box 149091, 111-1A
Austin, TX 78714-9091
512-463-6464

UTAH

Insurance Department
3110 State Office Building
Salt Lake City, UT 84114
801-530-3800

VERMONT

Insurance Department
89 Main St.
Drawer 20
Montpelier, VT 05620-3101
802-828-3301

VIRGINIA

Insurance Department
Bureau of Insurance
P.O. Box 1157
Richmond, VA 23218
804-371-9741

VIRGIN ISLANDS

Insurance Department
Lieutenant Governor's Office
18 Kongens Gade
St. Thomas, VI 00802
809-774-2991

WASHINGTON

Insurance Department
Insurance Commissioner
Insurance Building
P.O. Box 40255
Olympia, WA 98504-0255
360-753-7301

WEST VIRGINIA

Insurance Department
Department of Insurance
2019 Washington St. E.
Charleston, WV 25305
304-558-3393

WISCONSIN

Insurance Department
Commissioner of Insurance
121 E. Wilson St.
P.O. Box 7873
Madison, WI 53707-7873
608-266-3585

WYOMING

Insurance Department
Office of the Commissioner
Herschler Building,
   Third Floor East
122 W. 25th St.
Cheyenne, WY 82002-0440
307-777-7401

APPENDIX D

Health Insurance Information and Counseling

*E*very state—plus Puerto Rico, the Virgin Islands and the District of Columbia—has a health insurance counseling program that can give you free information and assistance on Medicare, Medicaid, Medigap, long-term-care and other health insurance benefits. You can call your state counseling office and ask for the names of health maintenance organizations in your area. Phone numbers are listed below (the 800 number works only within the state). If you have trouble reaching your counseling office, call the Medicare hotline at 800-638-6833.

Alabama 800-243-5463

Alaska 800-478-6065

Arizona 800-432-4040

Arkansas 800-852-5494

California 800-434-0222

Colorado 800-544-9181

Connecticut 800-994-9422

Delaware 800-336-9500

District of Columbia 202-676-3900

Florida 800-963-5337

Georgia 800-669-8387

Hawaii 808-586-0100

Idaho 800-488-5725

Illinois 800-548-9034

Indiana 800-452-4800

Iowa 800-351-4664

Kansas 800-432-3535

Kentucky 800-372-2973

Louisiana 800-259-5301

Maine 800-750-5353

Maryland 800-243-3425

Massachusetts 800-882-2003

Michigan 800-803-7174

Minnesota 800-882-6262

Mississippi 800-948-3090

Missouri 800-390-3330

Montana 800-332-2272

Nebraska 402-471-2201

Nevada 800-307-4444

New Hampshire 800-852-3388

New Jersey 800-792-8820

New Mexico 800-432-2080

New York 800-333-4114

North Carolina 800-443-9354

North Dakota 800-247-0560

Ohio 800-686-1578

Oklahoma 800-763-2828

Oregon 800-722-4134

Pennsylvania 800-783-7067

Puerto Rico 809-721-8590

Rhode Island 800-322-2880

South Carolina 800-868-9095

South Dakota 800-822-8804

Tennessee 800-525-2816

Texas 800-252-3439

Utah 800-439-3805

Vermont 802-828-3302

Virginia 800-552-3402

Virgin Islands 809-774-2991

Washington 800-397-4422

West Virginia 800-642-9004

Wisconsin 800-242-1060

Wyoming 800-856-4398

GLOSSARY

Accreditation: A process by which managed care plans are reviewed and evaluated by independent, outside organizations such as the National Committee for Quality Assurance. Accreditation measures how plans perform against national standards and against other managed care plans. Successful plans are accredited for a specific period of time and have to be reevaluated periodically to keep their accreditation.

Acute illness: An illness that occurs suddenly and is generally limited in its duration, but not necessarily in its severity or impact. Examples of acute illnesses include common colds, broken bones, heart attacks and food poisoning.

Admitting privileges: Permission granted by a hospital to certain doctors to admit patients to the hospital. Privileges are granted after the hospital checks the physician's qualifications. Hospitals can suspend privileges as a way of reprimanding a physician who provides poor-quality care or violates other hospital rules.

Alternative health care: Therapies such as chiropractic, acupuncture, naturopathy and homeopathy provided by physicians and nonphysicians trained in these fields.

Ancillary services: Additional health-care services, such as physical, occupational and speech therapy, that help speed recovery from an illness or injury. These services are typically provided upon the recommendation or prescription of a physician.

Appeal: A second level of review of a consumer's complaint by a managed care plan, after the plan was unable to address the problem to the consumer's satisfaction in an initial review.

Board certified: A term used to describe a physician who has passed an examination given by a medical specialty board and who has been certified as a specialist in that medical area. Doctors can be board certified in 24 different medical specialties recognized by the American Board of Medical Specialties.

Board eligible: A term used to describe a physician who is eligible to take a specialty board examination because she has graduated from an approved medical school, completed specific training in her field and practiced for a specific amount of time.

Capitation: A fixed monthly payment to a managed care plan by an employer or to a group of physicians by a managed care plan. The plan or the physicians are responsible for providing or arranging to provide all health-care services required by covered people under the conditions of the provider contracts.

Care pathways: Medical "road maps" set up by managed care plans and health-care providers (such as physicians' groups and hospitals) to help guide the care of individual consumers. A care pathway provides guidance on what services a consumer should receive at a particular point in his care, from whom and for how long.

Carve out: A situation in which managed care services, such as prescription drug benefits and vision benefits, are provided by companies specializing in them. Carve outs are generally organized and delivered by companies that are separate from the managed care plan that provides coverage for general medical care.

Chronic illness: An illness that is lengthy in duration (in some cases, a lifelong problem) and requires consistent monitoring and care. Examples of chronic illnesses include diabetes, heart disease, arthritis and glaucoma.

Claim: Information that a provider or consumer submits to her insurance plan to establish that medical services were provided to the person and from which processing for payment to the provider or consumer is made.

Claim form: Paperwork that a consumer files with a managed care plan to receive payment from the plan after treatment by a physician or hospital.

Clinical trial: A medical research study in which patients receive one of two treatments that are being compared with one another. The study may compare two existing treatments to each other to see which works better, a new treatment to an existing treatment or a new treatment to a placebo (inactive treatment). Patients must give their informed consent prior to joining a clinical trial and meet specific clinical criteria to be considered eligible.

Closed panel: A type of HMO—typically staff model—in which consumers are required to select doctors from the plan's list of participating providers. In this type of plan, the providers have exclusive contracts with the HMO.

Coinsurance: A cost-sharing requirement in many health insurance plans in which the consumer assumes a portion or percentage of the costs of covered services. Coinsurance often applies after the person has first met a deductible requirement.

Copayment: A cost-sharing requirement in which a consumer pays a specified charge for a specified health-care service, such as $5 for a doctor's office visit.

Credentialing: A process that managed care plans use to review the qualifications of physicians who work with the plans. Plans that seek to be accredited by organizations such as the National Committee for Quality Assurance must maintain a thorough credentialing process that checks education and training, board certification and disciplinary and malpractice history.

Customer service: A department within a managed care plan that answers consumers' questions, provides information about plan procedures and fields consumer grievances.

Deductible: The amount of money that a consumer must pay out-of-pocket each year before his insurance plan will make payments for eligible benefits.

Denial of care: Refusal by a physician in a managed care plan or the plan administration to pay for care that the consumer believes is indicated or medically necessary in a specific situation. An example of denial of care is refusal by a plan to refer a consumer to a specialist.

Discounted fee-for-service: A payment system in which physicians and hospitals accept less money than they typically would receive for providing care to consumers.

Disease management program: A coordinated program of care offered by some managed care plans that integrates testing, treatment and health education. Disease management programs aim to improve consumers' understanding of their ailments and their treatments and to help direct consumers to the right resources in the plan at the right time to ensure that treatment is as cost effective as possible.

Emergency care: Medical services that are required immediately after the onset of an illness to treat severe symptoms or a potentially life-threatening situation.

ERISA (Employee Retirement Income Security Act): A federal law under which employers operate and offer to their employees self-insured health insurance plans. The law includes reporting and disclosure requirements for group life and health plans.

Evidence of coverage: Managed care plan materials sent to a consumer after enrollment in the plan that provide detailed information on what services the plan covers and at what cost.

Experimental: Refers to tests, procedures and drugs whose safety and effectiveness have not been proven through well-designed studies such as clinical trials.

Family physician: A physician who provides a wide range of general medical care, including gynecologic and obstetric care, minor surgery, orthopedics and preventive medicine.

Fee-for-service: The traditional health-care payment system in which health-care providers, including physicians and hospitals, are paid after they provide services to consumers. Studies show that fee-for-service payment encourages over-use of medical care.

Fee schedule: A comprehensive list of amounts paid to physicians or hospitals on a fee-for-service basis. In any given situation, the amount paid depends on the complexity of the service provided, with more complex services paid at higher rates.

Formulary: An exclusive list of prescription drugs that are approved for use and/or coverage by the managed care plan or pharmacy benefit manager.

Gag rules: Contractual restrictions between a managed care plan and a physician that are intended to keep private the relationship between the managed care plan and the doctor. Gag rules can limit the information that consumers learn about arrangements for payment to physicians, such as bonuses for making fewer referrals to specialists. They may also restrict physicians from telling consumers the full range of treatment or testing options available to them.

Gatekeeper: The role played by primary care physicians in managed care plans to control how consumers use other services in the plans. Gatekeepers control consumers' access to hospitals, specialists and testing services.

General practitioner: A physician who, like a family physician, provides a wide range of general medical care to children and adults.

Generic drug: A drug whose active ingredients duplicate those of the brand-name product and whose name is usually a condensed version of the drug's original chemical name. While a generic drug does not have to be the same size, shape or color of the brand name, by law it does have to be bioequivalent. Sometimes generic drugs are less expensive than their brand-name counterparts.

Geriatrician or gerontologist: A physician who specializes in the medical care of older people.

Grievance: A consumer complaint against a managed care plan. All managed care plans have a grievance- or complaint-resolution process by which they review and address consumer grievances.

Group model HMO: A type of HMO that usually signs a contract with one or more large groups of physicians to provide care to HMO members. These doctors are not salaried employees of the HMO but are employed by their groups.

Health maintenance organization (HMO): A form of managed care; generally the most restrictive type of managed care plan, in which a consumer selects a physician gatekeeper who controls her access to other members in the HMO's network of doctors and hospitals. The HMO agrees to cover all of its members' health-care needs in exchange for a fixed, prepaid premium from employers and consumers.

Hospice care: Palliative and supportive care of the terminally ill and their families until the patient's death. The goal of hospice is to keep the patient as comfortable as possible through the last stages of his illness.

Independent practice association (IPA): A type of HMO in which the plan's administrators sign contracts with large numbers of physicians—both solo practice doctors and doctors in group practices—to provide care to the HMO members. Physicians in an IPA agree to a negotiated set of fees paid by the plan.

Inpatient: A consumer who is admitted to a hospital or other health-care facility for at least an overnight stay.

Internist: A physician who specializes in internal medicine. These doctors typically provide less pediatric, obstetric and gynecologic care than do family physicians.

License: An authorization by a state government agency (such as the health department) that a health-care provider has met the basic legal requirements in the state to render health-care services to consumers.

Malpractice: Injurious, negligent or otherwise improper medical care. Physicians can be sued for malpractice and can also have their licenses and hospital admitting privileges suspended or revoked.

Managed care: A system of health-care delivery that links payment with the delivery of health-care services with the aim of giving people access to quality, cost-effective health care. In managed care, the plan receives a fixed monthly payment from consumers and their employer to provide care to consumers in the plan.

Managed indemnity plan: A kind of managed care in which traditional fee-for-service indemnity insurance is combined with utilization review.

Medicaid: A joint federal and state government program that provides limited health insurance benefits to persons with low incomes who meet state-specific eligibility criteria.

Medicaid HMO: An HMO approved by a state government to enroll and care for Medicaid beneficiaries.

Medical director: In the context of managed care, a physician who is employed by a managed care plan and oversees other physicians who work with the plan. The medical director is also responsible for participating in technology assessment in the plan, as well as in the work of other committees that help decide what new treatments and tests to cover for plan members.

Medical licensing board: A regulatory agency in each state that provides physicians with licenses to practice medicine in that state. The medical licensing board also has the legal authority to punish physicians who violate physician practice laws by assaulting, defrauding or harming their patients. Punishment can include suspending or revoking the license to practice medicine.

Medical loss ratio: The amount of money that a managed care plan spends on health-care services (such as hospital and physician care) for plan members in relation to the amount it took in through premiums from employers and consumers.

Medically necessary: A determination by a managed care plan that a particular test or treatment is appropriate for a specific ailment. Managed care plans will cover and pay for care that is medically necessary.

Medically unnecessary: A determination by a managed care plan that a particular test or treatment is not appropriate for a specific ailment. Managed care plans will not cover or pay for care that they determine is medically unnecessary.

Medical record: A document maintained in a hospital or physician's office that contains a consumer's health-care history, including illnesses, tests, treatments, outcomes and communications between the health-care provider, consumer and health plan.

Medicare: The federally administered health insurance program that covers the cost of hospitalization, medical care and some related services for eligible persons, primarily those 65 years of age and older.

Medicare HMO: An HMO approved by the federal government to enroll and care for Medicare beneficiaries.

Mental health care: Services that diagnose and treat mental illness, including depression and bipolar disorder, using a combination of counseling, medication and other approaches.

Mixed model (or **network**) **HMO:** A type of HMO that has a mix of all the other models in one plan. The HMO contracts with solo physicians, groups of physicians and single- and multispecialty groups. The HMO may also employ some doctors.

Morbidity rates: Statistics that indicate how frequently consumers experience complications or side effects as a result of specific ailments, tests or treatments. Morbidity rates are expressed as numbers—such as the number of complications per 1,000 consumers with the ailment or undergoing the test or treatment—or as percentages.

Mortality rates: Statistics that indicate how frequently consumers die as a result of a particular disease, test or treatment. Mortality rates are usually expressed as the number of deaths per 1,000 consumers or as percentages (for example, 10 percent of consumers who undergo a specific procedure die as a result).

Networks of health-care providers: Groups of doctors, hospitals and other health-care providers who contract with managed care plans to care for consumers in the plans.

Nurse-midwives: Registered nurses with advanced training in the care of pregnant women. Nurse-midwives can provide prenatal care and deliver babies and often work with obstetrician/gynecologists.

Nurse practitioner: A registered nurse who has received advanced training in general medicine and can provide children and adults a wide range of basic health-care services. Nurse practitioners often work in teams with physicians, although in many states they are able to work as independently licensed health-care providers.

Obstetrician/gynecologist: A physician who specializes in women's health.

Ombudsman: A troubleshooter who helps consumers resolve their complaints with managed care plans. Some states are setting up ombudsman programs to help their Medicaid HMO enrollees work on complaint resolution.

Open enrollment: A period during which plan members have an opportunity to select an alternate health plan being offered to them. Typically, when enrollment takes place during this time, the consumer does not have to show evidence of insurability or observe a waiting period before becoming eligible for plan benefits.

Open panel: A managed care plan in which the physicians see consumers from a number of different managed care plans.

Ophthalmologist: A physician who specializes in the diagnosis and treatment of eye diseases. Ophthalmologists can prescribe drugs and perform surgical procedures, such as cataract extractions.

Optician: A nonphysician health-care professional who makes, fits and adjusts corrective lenses.

Optometrist: A nonphysician health-care professional who examines the eyes for eye diseases such as glaucoma and vision problems and prescribes eyeglasses and contact lenses.

Outcomes data: Information that tells how well consumers did after receiving a particular treatment or procedure. Outcomes data help consumers, plans and health-care providers understand what difference interventions made in the consumers' health care and quality of life.

Out-of-pocket: The portion of payments for health services required to be paid by the consumer, including copayments, monthly premiums and deductibles.

Outpatient: A consumer who is not admitted to a hospital for an overnight stay but who is treated in other health-care settings. Outpatient care is provided in clinics, hospital outpatient departments and physicians' offices.

Pediatrician: A physician who specializes in the care of children from birth to young adulthood.

Pharmacy and therapeutics committee: A group of managed care plan health-care professionals, such as physicians and pharmacists, who assess new drugs for coverage by the plan.

Pharmacy benefit manager (PBM): A company that specializes in managing prescription drug benefits in managed care.

Physician assistant: A health-care provider who typically has two years of intensive medical training and can provide a wide range of health-care services to consumers. In most states, physician assistants must work under the supervision of licensed physicians.

Physician hospital organization (PHO): A type of managed care plan that is owned and marketed by the doctors and hospitals who comprise the plan. The most recent addition to managed care and still relatively few in number, PHOs can market themselves directly to employers and consumers, as well as to other managed care plans to care for their consumer members. PHOs are also known as community health networks and provider-sponsored networks.

Point-of-service (POS): A type of managed care plan that is a hybrid of an HMO and traditional indemnity insurance. POS is one of the most rapidly growing forms of managed care. Consumers can choose a provider in the plan's network of providers and have lower out-of-pocket costs or use a provider outside the network at higher costs.

Practice profiling: A system used by a managed care plan to evaluate how its physicians practice medicine. A plan measures whether the way the physician practices is consistent with her peers or whether the physician makes too many referrals to specialists, orders too many tests or admits too many patients to the hospital. Practice profiling can affect whether a physician receives an annual bonus from the plan or her contract is renewed.

Preapproval: A process by which a managed care plan reviews and authorizes a procedure, test or treatment for a consumer before the care is rendered.

Precertification: Prior approval of a medical service, surgical procedure or nonemergency hospitalization by a managed care plan, based on the medical necessity and appropriateness of the service.

Preferred provider organization (PPO): A managed care plan with a large network of physicians, hospitals and other providers. A PPO offers consumers a wider choice of doctors and hospitals than does an HMO.

Premature hospital discharge: Termination of a hospital stay before the consumer and his physician believe it is appropriate to end the stay and send the consumer home.

Premium: The amount paid periodically by employers and consumers to insurance plans to be enrolled in the plans.

Preventive health care: Services and education that seek to keep health-care problems from developing (for example, weight-loss and exercise programs to reduce the risk of heart disease).

Primary care physician: A physician trained in one of the following fields of medicine, to provide a wide range of general medical care: family medicine, internal medicine, pediatrics, obstetrics and gynecology, geriatrics or gerontology. Primary care physicians play a key role in managed care, helping consumers identify and use other services in the plan.

Prior authorization: Prior approval by a managed care plan of a specialty referral, drug or other medical service or surgical procedure. The plan's prior authorization does not guarantee coverage or payment for the service by the plan.

Provider: A health-care professional (such as a physician, physician assistant, nurse practitioner or dentist) or facility (such as a hospital) that is properly licensed or certified to care for consumers.

Referral: Authorization by a managed care plan or a primary care physician for a consumer to see a specialist or use another service in the plan.

Report cards: Data on how managed care plans compare with one another and to national standards along specific criteria. Reports cards are being developed by managed care plans, state governments and independent organizations such as the National Committee for Quality Assurance to help employers and consumers judge managed care plans within specific quality-of-care criteria.

Screening tests: Medical procedures ordered or performed by physicians that seek to identify problems in their earliest possible stages of development, when they are easier and less expensive to treat.

Self-insured managed care plan: A managed care plan, owned and operated by an employer, that is subject to federal laws.

Shared financial risk: A process by which doctors and hospitals who contract with managed care plans find themselves sharing the costs of the services they provide. The goal of shared financial risk is to encourage health-care providers to be more efficient and to reduce the use of unnecessary services.

Sign: A manifestation of a disease that a physician can observe or measure during a physical exam, such as a rapid heartbeat or reddened skin.

Specialist: A physician who has elected to practice—and who usually has special training in—some branch of medicine other than primary care, such as surgery, or an exclusive focus in one area of primary care, such as allergy.

Staff model HMO: A type of HMO that employs physicians and pays them salaries. The physicians may also receive bonuses if the HMO does well financially. Typically, the staff model HMO owns the clinics and offices where consumers receive services.

Stop-loss insurance: Insurance purchased by health-care providers, such as physicians, physicians' groups, hospitals and physician hospital organizations, that helps limit the amount of money the provider can lose on the care of a consumer. Stop-loss insurance starts paying the health-care costs of an individual consumer after the provider has spent a predetermined sum.

Subspecialty certification: Certification conferred upon a physician who completes additional training beyond medical school and basic residency and develops detailed expertise in a narrowly focused area of medicine, such as pediatric cardiology.

Symptom: A manifestation of a disease that a patient can express to a physician, such as a headache or depression.

Technology assessment: The process by which a managed care plan, usually through the medical director's office, evaluates new treatments and tests to decide which ones the plan will cover and pay for.

Third-party administrator (TPA): A company that helps employers offering self-insured managed care plans run and manage the plans. The TPA administers benefits in the plans, manages cash flow and contracts with doctors and hospitals.

Traditional indemnity insurance: A health insurance plan that pays doctors and hospitals on a fee-for-service basis, after the consumer receives care, with little oversight to assess whether the care is medically necessary and appropriate.

Triage: A decision-making system that helps prioritize which consumers have the most severe illnesses and require immediate medical attention and which ones can wait.

Utilization review (UR): An oversight process in which the managed care plan reviews what services consumers received, how frequently and at what cost. Used most often with managed indemnity plans, UR programs are tools to control costs.

Well-baby (or **well-child**) **care:** Routine care for babies and children from birth through young adulthood that allows family physicians and pediatricians to monitor the overall health and development of children and deliver necessary services, such as immunizations.

INDEX

A

AAHC. *See* American Accreditation Healthcare Commission (AAHC)

Abortion, communication about, 114, 122

Accreditation
Accreditation Status List (ASL), 74
Accreditation Summary Report (ASR), 74
American Accreditation Healthcare Commission (AAHC), 70-72, 76-77, 90
defined, 42, 71, 207
Joint Commission on Accreditation of Healthcare Organizations (JCAHO), 70-72, 74-76, 77, 90
managed care plan, 70-77
National Committee for Quality Assurance (NCQA), 70-74, 77, 90

Accreditation Status List (ASL), defined, 74

Accreditation Summary Report (ASR), defined, 74

Acquired immunodeficiency syndrome (AIDS). *See* AIDS

Acupuncture, coverage, 161-162

Acute illness
coverage, 134-136, 148
defined, 134, 207
referrals and, 135-136

Administration
medical loss ratio and, 59, 85, 91
role, 55-56

Admitting privileges
defined, 207
hospitals not covered and, 143
verification, 111-112, 115, 121

Advertising, medical loss ratio and, 59, 85, 91

Aetna-US Healthcare, profits and, 58

AIDS
  clinical trials and, 84
  prescription drug coverage and,
    156-157
Allied health-care professionals,
  managed care and, 43-44
Alternative health care
  coverage, 161-162
  defined, 151, 208
American Accreditation
  Healthcare Commission
  (AAHC)
  accreditation process, 70-72,
    76-77, 77, 90
  authority, 71
  board of directors, 76-77
Ancillary services, defined,
  160, 208
Anemia, sickle-cell
  changing care plans and, 68
  screening tests, 133
Angiograms, surgeon experience
  level and, 117
Appeal, defined, 37, 208
Arthritis, coverage, 136
Asthma, coverage, 79, 136,
  137, 148

B

Billing problems, managed care
  and, 79-80, 90, 163, 166
Blood pressure
  coverage, 79, 136
  managed care and, 26-27, 96
Board certified
  American Board of Medical
    Specialties (ABMS), 110
  defined, 107, 208
  specialty areas, 110, 115-115
  subspecialty certification,
    110, 223

verification, 107-109, 110,
  115, 121
Board eligible, defined, 108
Bonus, annual, physicians and,
  100-101, 123, 145
Braces, coverage, 155
Breast cancer, managed care and,
  48, 57, 133, 145

C

Cancer
  breast, managed care and,
    48, 57, 133, 145
  clinical trials and, 84
  screening tests, coverage,
    78, 133
Capitation
  defined, 35, 99, 208
  laboratory tests and, 100
  referrals and, 100
  stop-loss insurance and, 64,
    100, 123
  x-rays and, 100
Cardiologists
  interventional, experience level,
    117, 143, 144
  primary care physicians vs., 119
Care pathways
  defined, 43, 209
  managed care and, 43, 61, 209
Carve outs
  defined, 128, 129-130, 209
  mental health benefits, 129,
    151-153
  prescription drugs, 129,
    155-157
  vision and dental care, 130
Cataracts
  extraction, 117, 133
  screening tests, 133

Childbirth, hospital discharge
after, 56-57, 144-146
Children
chronic illness and, 68
dependent children living away
from home, 158-159
managed care and, 148-149
screening tests, 133
Chiropractic, coverage, 161-162
Cholesterol screening, coverage,
48, 133
Chronic illness
changing care plans and, 68,
79-81
children and, 68
defined, 68, 136, 209
managed care and, 53, 68,
79-81, 90, 96, 119,
136-139
specialists vs. primary care
physicians and, 119,
138-139, 148-149
Claim, defined, 31, 209
Claim forms, defined, 52, 209
Clinical trials
AIDS and, 84
coverage, 84, 91
defined, 84, 209-210
Closed panel, defined, 34, 210
Coinsurance, defined, 210
Colon cancer, screening tests, 133
Communication, patients and
physicians and, 106-107
Competition, managed care,
60-61
Complaints
customer service department,
164-166
grievance preparation
guidelines, 167-175

Medicaid health maintenance
organizations (HMOs),
175-176
Medicare health maintenance
organizations (HMOs),
173-175
procedure, 79
reasons for, 79
sample complaint letter,
170-172
self-insured managed care plan
and, 177-179
state regulatory agencies and,
90, 164
written complaint guidelines,
166-167
Computer networks, medical
records and, 102
Conflict of interest, managed care
and, 28, 29, 54-55
Consumer complaints
customer service department,
164-166
grievance preparation
guidelines, 167-175
managed care, 79, 90
Medicaid health maintenance
organizations (HMOs),
175-176
Medicare health maintenance
organizations (HMOs),
173-175
reasons for, 79
sample complaint letter,
170-172
self-insured managed care plan
and, 177-179
state regulatory agencies and,
164
written complaint guidelines,
166-167

Consumer satisfaction
   doctor-patient relationship and,
      67-68, 96
   guidelines, 181-183
   surveys, 183
Contact lenses, coverage, 78
Contraception
   communication about, 114
   foams/gels/suppositories,
      coverage, 133
   implantable, coverage, 132
   injectable, coverage, 132
   surgical, coverage, 132
Coordination of care, managed
   care and, 47-48, 118-119,
   162
Copayments
   defined, 24, 45, 210
   Medicare health maintenance
      organizations (HMOs)
      and, 37
   mental health care and, 152
   prescription drugs and, 155-156
Coronary bypass surgery,
   surgery team experience and,
   117, 143
Costs, managed care and, 41
Credentialing, defined, 76-77,
   105, 210
Cultural factors, communication
   with physicians and, 106-107
Customer service, defined,
   126-127, 210

D
Deductibles
   defined, 24, 45, 210
   mental health care and, 152
Denial of care, defined, 79, 211
Denial of treatment
   experimental, 163

physician aid and, 101, 136
Dental care
   carve outs and, 130
   managed care and, 151, 153,
      154-155
Depo-Provera, coverage, 132
Diabetes
   coverage, 79, 96, 136, 137
   managed care and, 38
Diagnostic tests, precertification,
   40, 220
Diaphragm, coverage, 132-133
Disciplinary history, verification,
   112, 115, 121
Discounted fee-for-service,
   defined, 98, 99, 211
Disease detection, early, managed
   care and, 48
Disease management programs,
   defined, 43, 211
Disputes. See also Consumer
   complaints
   consumer, 79-80, 163-179
Divorce, dependent children living
   away from home, 158-159
DOL. See U.S. Department of
   Labor (DOL)
Drugs. See Prescription drugs

E
Emergency care, defined,
   126, 211
Emergency care hotline,
   defined, 126
Emergency room visits, health
   maintenance organizations
   (HMOs) and, 50-51, 93,
   140-142
Employee Retirement Income
   Security. See ERISA

Employers, managed care and, 65-66
Enrollment period, defined, 66
ERISA
    defined, 86, 211
    preventive health care and, 131
    self-insured managed care plan and, 178-179
Evidence of coverage, defined, 127, 211
Executive salaries, medical loss ratio and, 85
Experimental, defined, 163, 212
Eye exams, coverage, 78
Eyeglasses, coverage, 78

F

Family physician, defined, 25, 103, 212
Fee-for-service. *See also* Traditional indemnity insurance
    defined, 21, 99, 212
    discounted, defined, 98, 99, 211
Fee schedule, defined, 98, 99, 212
Financial risk, managed care and, 62-64, 123
For-profit managed care plans, not-for-profit vs., 57-60
Formulary
    defined, 132, 164, 212
    prescription drug coverage and, 156

G

Gag rules
    defined, 27-28, 212
    laws about, 29
Gatekeeper, defined, 32, 213
General practitioner, defined, 103, 213

Generic drug, defined, 156, 213
Geriatrician, defined, 104, 213
Gerontologist, defined, 104, 213
Glaucoma
    managed care and, 38, 47, 133
    screening tests, 133
Grievance procedure, defined, 79, 213
Grievances
    denial referrals, 79, 136, 163, 164, 166-175
    Medicaid health maintenance organizations (HMOs), 175-176
    Medicare health maintenance organizations (HMOs), 173-175
    preparation guidelines, 167-175
    sample complaint letter, 170-172
    second opinions and, 168
    self-insured managed care plan and, 177-179
    written complaint guidelines, 166-167
Gum disease, coverage, 155
Gynecologic care
    coverage, 131
    referrals and, 131

H

Health-care professionals, managed care and allied, 43-44
Health-care providers, managed care effects, 60-64
Health education programs
    coverage, 133-134
    health maintenance organizations (HMOs) and, 48, 52

Health Insurance Employer Data
    Information Set (HEDIS),
    National Committee for
    Quality Assurance (NCQA)
    and, 73-74
Health insurance information
    and counseling, contact
    information, 203-205
Health maintenance organizations
    (HMOs)
    advantages, 45-52
    billing problems, 79-80, 90
    cancer screenings, 78
    changing physicians, 81-82
    children and, 148-149
    choosing a physician, 97
    chronic illness, 53, 79-81, 90,
        139
    copayments, 45, 92-93
    credentialing process, 105-106
    defined, 22, 30, 213-214
    disease management programs,
        43, 211
    early disease detection, 48
    emergency room visits, 50-51,
        93, 140-142
    employers and, 65-66
    evaluation checklist, 89-93
    expenses, out-of-pocket, 45, 46,
        48-49
    group model, defined, 34-35,
        213
    health education and wellness
        programs, 48, 52
    hospital services, 142
    independent practice association
        (IPA), defined, 35, 214
    individual enrollees, 66
    Medicaid, 30, 31, 36, 38-39,
        53, 66, 146, 175, 215

Medicare, 30, 31, 36-37, 53,
    66, 100, 146, 156,
    173-175, 216
mixed model, defined, 35-36,
    217
network, defined, 35-36, 217
occupational therapy and
    Medicare, 174
paperwork, 52
physical therapy and Medicare,
    174
physician and hospital
    efficiency and, 42-44
physician hospital organizations
    (PHOs) and, 61-63
physician turnover rates, 109
pregnancy and, 147
prenatal care, 78
prescription drug coverage, 49,
    155-157
preventive health care, 48, 52,
    78, 130
primary care physician and,
    102-103
pros and cons, generally, 44-45
referral to specialist options,
    115
report cards, 42-43, 69, 92, 222
retirees' health care away from
    home and, 159
screening tests, 133
self-employment/small business
    and, 66
self-insured managed care plan
    and, 86-87, 92, 222
speech therapy and Medicare,
    174
staff model, defined, 34, 223
treatment decisions, 84
vision care, 78
well-baby care, 30, 78

Health Net, profits and, 57
Heart disease
  clinical trials and, 84
  coverage, 79, 136, 137
  managed care and, 48
Heart surgery, program
  comparison, 144
HMOs. *See* Health maintenance
  organizations (HMOs)
Home care
  coverage, 78
  hospice care and, 161
  hospitalization vs., 146
Homeopathy, coverage, 161
Hospice care
  coverage, 160-161
  defined, 37, 214
  Medicare and, 37
  Medicare health maintenance
    organizations (HMOs)
    and, 160
Hospital discipline, verification,
  112, 115, 121
Hospital services, coverage,
  142-146
Hospitalization
  admitting privileges, 111-112,
    115, 121, 143
  discharge after childbirth,
    56-57, 144-146
  health maintenance organi-
    zations (HMOs) and
    efficiency, 42
  preapproval, 40, 220
  premature discharge, 56-57,
    144-146, 164
Hotline
  customer service, 126
  emergency care, 126, 141
Hypertension. *See* Blood pressure

I

Illnesses away from home,
  managed care and, 157-159
Immunizations, coverage, 48, 148
Individual enrollees, managed care
  and, 66
Information sources
  health insurance information
    and counseling, 203-205
  state attorney generals' offices,
    185-190
  state health departments,
    191-196
  state insurance departments,
    197-202
Informed choices, gag rules and,
  27-28, 29
Injuries away from home, managed care and, 157-159
Inpatient, defined, 35, 214
Insurance
  state insurance departments.
    See also State regulatory
    agencies
  contact information, 197-202
  stop-loss, defined, 64, 100, 223
Internet, medical records and, 102
Internist, defined, 32, 103, 214
Interview appointments, physicians and, 113-114, 122
Intravenous pumps, coverage, 78

J

JCAHO. *See* Joint Commission on
  Accreditation of Healthcare
  Organizations (JCAHO)
Joint Commission on
  Accreditation of Healthcare
  Organizations (JCAHO)
  accreditation process, 70-72,
    75-76, 77, 90

authority, 71
Joint replacement surgery, surgery
   team experience and, 117

L

Labor and delivery, coverage, 147
Laboratory tests
   capitation and, 100
   coverage, 131
   physicians' financial interest in
      facilities, 113, 122
Licenses
   defined, 69-70, 214
   status, 107-108, 112, 115, 121

M

Malpractice
   defined, 105, 214
   physician profiles and, 112-113
   premature hospital discharge
      and, 146
Mammography, coverage, 48, 133
Managed care. *See also* Health
   maintenance organizations
   (HMOs); Managed indem-
   nity plans; Physician hospital
   organizations (PHOs); Point-
   of-Service (POS); Preferred
   provider organizations
   (PPOs)
   accreditation, 42, 70-77
   acute illnesses and, 134-136,
      148
   benefits, 41-44
   billing problems, 79-80, 90,
      163, 166
   care pathways, 43, 61, 209
   carve outs, 128, 129-130, 209
   choosing a physician, 96-98
   chronic illness and, 53, 68,
      79-81, 90, 96, 119, 137-139

clinical trials and, 84, 91
consumer complaints, 79, 90,
   164-179
contraception and, 132-133
controversies, 52-57
coordination of care, 47-48,
   118-119, 162
coping guidelines, 181-183
deductible, 45, 93
defined, 21, 22, 215
dental care and, 151, 153,
   154-155
doctor's contractual status, 109
effects, 26
effects on health-care providers,
   60-64
evaluation checklist, 89-93
goals, 22-23
goals in selecting, 67-68
grievances, 79, 136, 163, 164,
   166-175, 213
gynecologic care, 131
health education and, 48, 52,
   133-134
history, 25-26, 52-53
illnesses away from home and,
   157-159
injuries away from home and,
   157-159
long-term impacts, 52
mental health care, 151-153
outcomes data and, 42, 43, 102,
   118, 143-144
physical exams and, 131
predictions for future, 181-183
preventive health care, 23, 48,
   52, 78, 128, 130-134, 221
program types, 30-31
pros and cons, generally, 30,
   44-45

relationship between physicians
and, 98-102
report cards, 42-43, 69, 92, 222
satisfaction guidelines, 181-183
screening tests, 133
self-insured, defined, 86-87, 222
services provided by other
vendors, 127-128
shared financial risk, 62-64, 123
technology assessment and,
83-84
traditional indemnity insurance
vs., 21, 23, 28
traveling and, 157-159
treatment decisions, 83-84
vision care, 78, 151, 153-154
well-baby care, 30, 78, 131
well-child care, 131
Managed indemnity plans
balance negotiation, 97
cancer screenings, 78
changing physicians in, 52
children and, 149
choosing a physician, 97
copayments, 45, 92-93
defined, 39-40, 215
early disease detection, 48
emergency care, 140, 142
evaluation checklist, 89-93
expenses, out-of-pocket, 45,
46, 48-49
home care, 78
hospital services, 142
inefficiencies, 47-48
medical equipment, 78
mental health services, 78
occupational therapy, 78
paperwork, 52
physical therapy, 78
pregnancy and, 147
prenatal care, 78

prescription drug coverage, 51
preventive health care, 48, 78,
130
primary care physician and,
102-103
pros and cons, generally, 44-45
rehabilitation services, 78
retirees' health care away from
home and, 159
self-employment/small business
and, 66
self-insured managed care plan
and, 86, 92
substance abuse treatment, 78
treatment decisions and, 84
well-baby care, 78
Massage therapy, coverage, 162
Mastectomy, outpatient vs.
inpatient, 56-57, 145
Medi-Net, physician background
resources, 108
Medicaid, defined, 22, 215
Medical care, coordination of
care, 47-48, 118-119, 162
Medical centers, major
access, 91
benefits, 83
Medical director, defined, 82, 215
Medical equipment, coverage, 78
Medical licensing board
defined, 107, 215
hospital privileges and, 112
Medical loss ratio
defined, 57, 85, 216
for-profit vs. not-for-profit care
plans and, 57, 60
Medical records
defined, 47, 216
grievances and, 167-168
privacy issues, 102, 123

Medically necessary, defined,
    49, 216
Medically unnecessary, defined,
    163, 216
Medicare
    defined, 22, 216
    hotline, 174, 203
Medications. *See* Prescription
    drugs
    coverage, 43, 49, 51
Membership card, defined, 126
Mental health care
    carve outs and, 129, 152
    copayments and, 152
    deductibles and, 152
    defined, 78, 216
    managed care and, 151-153
    utilization review (UR) and,
        152-153
Mental health services, coverage,
    78
Monthly premium, defined, 45
Morbidity rates, defined, 143, 217
Mortality rates, defined, 143, 217
Multiphysician groups, specialists
    and, 82, 111, 149

N

National Committee for Quality
    Assurance (NCQA)
    accreditation process, 70-72,
        72-74, 77, 90
    authority, 71
    board of directors, 72
    HMO rating by, 42-43
    physician evaluation by, 105
Naturopathy, coverage, 161
NCQA. *See* National Committee
    for Quality Assurance
    (NCQA)

Networks of health-care providers,
    defined, 32, 217
Norplant, coverage, 132
Nurse-midwives, defined, 217
Nurse practitioner, defined,
    26, 217
Nutrition counseling, coverage, 48
Nutrition therapy, coverage, 162

O

Obstetrician/gynecologists,
    defined, 32, 104, 218
Occupational therapy, coverage,
    78, 174
Ombudsman
    defined, 39, 218
    Medicaid and, 39
Open enrollment, defined, 66, 218
Open heart surgery, program
    comparison, 144
Open panel, defined, 35, 218
Ophthalmologists
    defined, 33, 153, 218
    experience level, 117
    optometrists vs., 153-154
Opticians, defined, 130, 218
Optometrists
    defined, 130, 218
    ophthalmologists vs., 153-154
Oral surgery, coverage, 155
Orthodontics, coverage, 155
Out-of-pocket expenses
    defined, 27, 219
    managed care and, 45, 46,
        48-49
Outcomes data
    defined, 42, 43, 118, 219
    hospital services and, 143-144
    medical records and, 102
Outpatient, defined, 56, 219

P

Paperwork, managed care and, 52
Payment, physicians payment by
managed care, 98-102, 122
PBM. *See* Pharmacy benefit
manager (PBM)
Pediatric surgery, multiphysician
groups and, 82
Pediatricians
defined, 32, 103-104, 219
primary care physician vs.,
148-149
Periodontist, coverage, 155
Pharmacy and therapeutics
committees, defined, 83, 219
Pharmacy benefit manager (PBM)
defined, 49, 155, 219
exhausted benefits and, 157
retirees' health care away from
home and, 159
PHOs. *See* Physician hospital
organizations (PHOs)
Physical exams, coverage, 131
Physical therapy, coverage,
78, 174
Physician assistant, defined,
26, 219
Physician hospital organizations
(PHOs), defined, 30, 31,
61, 220
Physician-patient relationship
managed care effects, 95-96
plan satisfaction and, 67-68, 96
Physicians
board certified, 107-109, 110,
115, 121
changing, managed care and,
81-82
conflict of interest, 28, 29,
54-55

disciplinary history, 112, 115,
121
evaluation by National
Committee for Quality
Assurance (NCQA), 105
family, defined, 25, 212
health maintenance organizations (HMOs) and
efficiency, 42
internist, 32, 214
interview appointments and,
113-114, 122
obstetrician/gynecologist,
32, 218
payment by managed care,
98-102, 122
pediatrician, 32, 219
primary care
care coordination with
alternative medicine
specialist, 162
care coordination with
specialist, 118-119
defined, 24, 221
evaluation and selection
checklist, 121-123
pediatrician vs., 148-149
referrals and, 32, 33
role, 32-33, 47, 102-104
specialists vs., 119, 138-139,
148-149
switching, ease of, 90
transition guidelines, 120-123
types
family physician, 103
general practitioner, 103
geriatrician, 104
gerontologist, 104
internist, 103
obstetrician/gynecologist,
104

pediatrician, 103-104
relationship between managed
    care and, 98-102
teaching hospitals and, 113, 122
turnover rates, 109
Plan membership materials,
    defined, 127
Point-of-service (POS)
    balance negotiation, 97
    cancer screenings, 78
    children and, 148-149
    choosing a physician, 97
    credentialing process, 105-106
    defined, 30, 31, 33, 220
    early disease detection, 48
    emergency care, 142
    employers and, 65-66
    expenses, out-of-pocket, 45,
        46, 48-49
    home care, 78
    hospital services, 142
    inefficiencies, 47-48
    medical equipment and, 78
    mental health services, 78
    occupational therapy, 78
    paperwork, 52
    physical therapy, 78
    physician-patient relationship
        and, 68
    pregnancy and, 148
    prenatal care, 78
    preventive health care, 48,
        78, 130
    primary care physician and,
        102-103
    pros and cons, 31, 33-34
        generally, 44-45
    referral to specialist options,
        115
    rehabilitation services, 78

retirees' health care away from
    home and, 159
screening tests, 133
self-employment/small business
    and, 66
self-insured managed care plan
    and, 86, 92
substance abuse treatment, 78
vision care, 78
well-baby care, 78
POS. See Point-of-service (POS)
Postpartum care, coverage, 147
PPOs. See Preferred provider
    organizations (PPOs)
Practice profiling
    consumer communication,
        101, 123
    defined, 101, 220
Preapproval, defined, 40, 220
Precertification, defined, 40, 220
Preferred provider organizations
    (PPOs)
    cancer screenings, 78
    changing physicians in, 81-82
    children and, 148-149
    choosing a physician, 97
    copayments, 45, 92-93
    credentialing process, 105-106
    defined, 30-31, 221
    early disease detection, 48
    emergency care, 142
    employers and, 65-66
    evaluation checklist, 89-93
    expenses, out-of-pocket, 45,
        46, 48-49
    home care, 78
    hospital services, 142
    inefficiencies and, 47-48
    medical equipment and, 78
    mental health services, 78

occupational therapy, 78
paperwork, 52
physical therapy, 78
pregnancy and, 147
prenatal care, 78
prescription drug coverage, 51
preventive health care, 48,
   78, 130
primary care physician,
   102-103
pros and cons, generally, 44-45
referral to specialist options,
   115
rehabilitation services, 78
retirees' health care away from
   home and, 159
screening tests, 133
self-employment/small business
   and, 66
self-insured managed care plan
   and, 86, 92
substance abuse treatment, 78
vision care, 78
well-baby care, 78
Pregnancy, coverage, 147
Premature hospital discharge,
   consumer complaints about,
   144-146, 164
Premiums
   defined, 23, 221
   monthly, defined, 45
Prenatal care, coverage, 78, 147
Prescription drugs
   AIDS treatment, 156-157
   copayments and, 155-156
   coverage, 43, 49, 51, 78, 129,
      155-157, 173-174
   generic, 156, 213
   mail order, 156
   physician transition and drug
      reactions, 120

Preventive health care
   coverage, 48, 52, 78, 128,
      130-134
   defined, 23, 221
Primary care physician
   care coordination with alter-
      native medicine specialist,
      162
   changing, managed care and,
      81-82
   defined, 24, 221
   evaluation and selection
      checklist, 121-123
   pediatrician vs., 148-149
   referrals and, 32, 33
   role, 32-33, 47, 102-104
   specialists vs., 119, 138-139,
      148-149
   switching, ease of, 90
   transition guidelines, 120-123
   types
      family physician, 103
      geriatrician, 104
      gerontologist, 104
      internist, 103
      obstetrician/gynecologist, 104
      pediatrician, 103-104
Prior authorization, defined,
   40, 221
Profits
   for-profit vs. not-for-profit
      managed care plans,
      57-60
   medical loss ratio and, 85
   physicians' and practice profit-
      sharing, 100-101, 123
Prostate cancer, screening tests,
   133
Providers, defined, 24, 221

Q

Quality assurance, National Committee for Quality Assurance (NCQA), 42-43

R

Race, communication with physicians and, 106-107
Ranking, managed care plan, 69
Rectal cancer, screening tests, 133
Referral facilities, physicians' financial interest, 113, 122
Referrals
acute illnesses and, 135-136
capitation and, 100
defined, 23, 222
denial
grievance procedure and, 79, 136, 163, 164, 166-175
physician aid with, 101, 123, 136
gynecologic care and, 131
physician, 28
primary care physicians and, 32, 33
special limitations, 82
specialists, 115
Rehabilitation services, coverage, 78
Renal disease, end-stage, specialists vs. primary care physicians and, 119
Report cards, defined, 42, 222
Research, managed care and, 43
Retirees, health care away from home, 159

S

Salaries, executive, medical loss ratio and, 85

Satisfaction
doctor-patient relationship and, 67-68, 96
guidelines for consumer, 181-183
Scoliosis, screening tests, 133
Screening tests
coverage, 133
defined, 133, 222
Second opinions, grievances and, 168
Self-employment, managed care and, 66
Self-insured managed care plan
consumer complaints and, 178-180
defined, 86-87, 222
Shared financial risk, defined, 62-64, 123, 222
Shareholders' profits, medical loss ratio and, 85
Sickle-cell anemia
changing care plans and, 68
screening tests, 133
Signs, disease, defined, 116, 222
Small businesses, managed care and, 66
Smoking cessation programs, coverage, 133, 134
Specialists
access, managed care and, 81-82, 91, 164
board certification, 115-116, 121
care coordination with primary care doctor, 118-119
defined, 24, 223
evaluation and selection checklist, 121-123
experience level, 116-117, 122

invasive procedures and, 117
maintaining, 114-115
outcomes data and, 118
referral, 115
replacement, 115
switching, ease of, 90
training verification, 115
transition guidelines, 120-123
Specialty boards, certification, 110
State attorney generals' offices,
    contact information, 185-190
State health departments, contact
    information, 191-196
State insurance departments,
    contact information, 197-202
State regulatory agencies. *See also*
    State attorney generals'
    offices; State health depart-
    ments; State insurance
    departments
    consumer complaints and,
        176-178
    contraception and, 133
    managed care and, 69-70, 79,
        82
    Medicare grievances and, 174
    self-employment/small business
        and, 66
    special referral limitations and,
        82
Stop-loss insurance
    capitation and, 100, 123
    defined, 64, 100, 223
Stress management programs,
    coverage, 133
Subspecialty certification, defined,
    110, 223
Substance abuse treatment,
    coverage, 78
Suicide, physician-assisted,
    communication about, 114

Surgeons, experience level, 117,
    122, 143, 144
Surgery
    contraception, coverage, 132
    coronary bypass
        coverage, 143
        surgery team experience and,
            117
    joint replacement, surgery team
        experience and, 117
    open heart, program
        comparison, 144
    oral, coverage, 155
    outpatient vs. inpatient, 56-57
    surgery team experience, 117,
        122
    transplantation, surgery team
        experience and, 117
Symptoms, defined, 26, 223

T

Teaching, physicians and, 113,
    122
Technology assessment
    defined, 83, 223
    treatment decisions and, 83-84
Terminal illness, hospice care and,
    160-161
The American Medical Associa-
    tion (AMA), physician back-
    ground resources, 107-108
Third-party administrator (TPA),
    defined, 87, 224
TPA. *See* Third-party adminis-
    trator (TPA)
Traditional indemnity insurance
    defined, 21, 22, 23, 24, 224
    effects, 27
Traditional indemnity insurance
    with UR. *See* Managed
    indemnity plans

Transplantation, surgery team
  experience and, 117
Traveling, managed care and,
  157-159
Treatment
  decisions, medical director vs.
    committee, 83-84
  denial
    experimental, 163
    physician aid with, 101, 136
Triage, defined, 140, 224
Tubal ligation, coverage, 132

U

United HealthCare, profits and,
  57-58
UR programs. *See* Utilization
  review (UR)
Urinalysis, coverage, 131
U.S. Department of Labor (DOL),
  self-insured managed care
  plan and, 178-179
Utilization review (UR)
  defined, 39-40, 224
  emergency care and, 140
  mental health care and, 152-153

V

Vasectomy, coverage, 132
Vision care
  carve outs and, 130
  coverage, 78, 154
  managed care and, 78, 151,
    153-154
  ophthalmologist experience
    level and, 117

W

Weight loss programs, coverage,
  133
Well-baby care
  coverage, 30, 78, 131
  defined, 30, 224
Well-child care
  coverage, 131
  defined, 131, 224
Wellness programs, health
  maintenance organizations
  (HMOs) and, 48
Wheelchairs, coverage, 78

X

X-rays
  capitation and, 100
  physicians' financial interest in
    facilities, 113, 122